Also by Esther M. Berger

Money Smart: Secrets Women Need to Know About Money
(*with Connie Church Hasbun*)

MoneySmart
Divorce

WHAT WOMEN NEED TO KNOW ABOUT MONEY AND DIVORCE

• • •

Esther M. Berger, CFP

*First Vice President,
PaineWebber Incorporated*

Simon & Schuster

New York London Toronto Sydney Tokyo Singapore

SIMON AND SCHUSTER
Rockefeller Center
1230 Avenue of the Americas
New York, NY 10020

SIMON & SCHUSTER and colophon are registered trademarks of
Simon & Schuster Inc.

Designed by Chris Welch
Manufactured in the United States of America

3   5   7   9   10   8   6   4   2

Library of Congress Cataloging-in-Publication Data
Berger, Esther M.
MoneySmart divorce : what women need to know about money and divorce/
Esther M. Berger
p.   cm.
1. Divorce—Economic aspects—United States.
2. Divorced women—United States—Finance, Personal. I. Title.
HQ834.B46   1996
332.024'042—dc20   95-40056
ISBN 0-684-81165-0

Acknowledgments

My special thanks, first and foremost, to Stacy Kravetz. Stacy is both a gifted wordsmith and an extraordinarily hard worker with the amazing ability to not only organize massive amounts of material but also to decipher the hieroglyphics that pass for my handwritten notes. Talented, dedicated, and completely unflappable—even in the face of an earthquake—Stacy is a joy to work with and a pleasure to know. My thanks to Chris DuBrow for introducing her to me.

Dan Strone at the William Morris Agency is the best there is—literary agent *par excellence* and a true mensch. Bob Asahina and Sarah Pinckney at Simon & Schuster are smart, supportive, and blessedly gentle with a blue pencil.

My parents, Leonard and Susan Fuchs, taught me about ethics, honesty, and the value of being moneysmart.

Judge Christian Markey, Judge Jill Robbins, and Stacy D. Phillips, Esq., generously gave of their time and expertise and were invaluable resources in enhancing both the accuracy and real-life applicability of the legal information on these pages.

6   **Acknowledgments**

Attorneys Leah Bishop, Mark Hess, Alexandra Leichter, and Michael Maroko displayed their usual brilliance, patience, and good humor explaining the finer points of family law and estate planning to a non-lawyer in non-legalese.

Sharon Grinage shared with me her experiences and those of thousands of other divorced women. I will always admire her courage, and theirs. Nancy Abrams, CFP, Polina Jaeger, C.P.A., Virginia Knight, A.S.I.D., and Clara Zilberstein, Ph.D., are Renaissance women of the nineties and truly wonderful friends. Sandi Kantor has the special gift of embracing every day with joy and helping me do the same.

And, as always, among the many blessings in my life, those I am most grateful for are my guys: Michael, Jeffrey, David, and, most of all, Leon.

For my grandmother Cecilia, one of the smartest and most loving women I've ever known. I miss her wit, her wisdom, and her spirit.

Contents

*When Your Heart Falls in the Cuisinart . . . Overcoming
Emotional Paralysis: Making the First Phone Call . . . The
Initial Consultation: Questions to Ask . . . Going the
Lawyer Route . . . Accept No Less Than You
Deserve . . . Keeping Legal Costs Down . . . The Non-
Attorney Options. . . Your Divorce "A Team" . . . Getting
Your Ducks in a Row . . . And Don't Overlook . . . Get-
ting Down to Business . . . Home Sweet Home: Who
Moves Out and When? . . . Who Pays for What? . . . But
I'd Rather Be the One Who Moves Out . . . Financial
Repercussions of Separating . . . Credit Where It's
Due . . . How to Handle Joint Accounts . . . Equity Credit
Lines . . . Brokerage Accounts . . . Joint Bank*

*Accounts . . . Assessing Your State of Mind: Where Am I
Coming From? . . . Where Am I Going? . . . Getting Help
When You Need Help: Counseling . . . Attack of the Not-
So-Great Ideas*

*When Smoke Gets in Your Eyes . . . Moving
Forward . . . My Two C's and Two D's: A Money Philoso-
phy That Will Guide You Through Divorce and Through
Life . . . The First C: Common Sense . . . The Second C:
Comfort Zone . . . The First D: Diversification . . . The
Second D: Discipline . . . Your Five- and Ten-Year Life
Plan: How to Get Started . . . Making a Plan and Check-
ing It Twice . . . Just the Facts, Ma'am . . . Keeping It All
Together: Temporary Support . . . Supporting Your Chil-
dren . . . The Road to Discovery . . . What Exactly Is Dis-
covery? . . . Depositions, Interrogatories, and
Subpoenas . . . In What State Are Your Finances? What
You Get Depends on Where You Live . . . Community
Property . . . Equitable Distribution . . . Separating Yours,
Mine, and Ours . . . What You Owe: Liabilities . . . "Don't
Ask, Don't Tell" . . . Searching for Buried Treasure . . .
Digging Deeper . . . Following the Paper Trail . . . Snoopy
or Charlie Brown? . . . Keeping an Eye on the Bottom
Line . . . Be on the Lookout for These Divorce Dirty
Tricks . . . Insuring Your Well-being . . . Your Health
Checkup . . . Disability Coverage . . . Your Life and Your
Husband's*

*Who Owns What? Your Business Assets . . . What's the
Business Worth? . . . Are Two Heads Better Than
One? . . . The Business Bottom Line . . . Your House: Love*

PART IV. Resolution   151

MOVING FROM TWO TO ONE   153

PART V. Reentry   195

Around . . . Prenuptial Agreements . . . What Is a Prenup? . . . Will He Think I Don't Love Him? . . . Commingling Assets . . . Postnuptial Agreements . . . Financially Happily Ever After

Introduction: Why You Need a MoneySmart Divorce

The ink was barely dry on her divorce papers when my client, Jaynie, hightailed it out of Los Angeles and moved to Pennsylvania with her nine-year-old daughter, Charlene. What was the big rush? Bottom line: Jaynie just couldn't stand the thought of living in the same city as her ex-husband and his cute-as-a-button secretary who would soon become wife number two. "It was like a bad storyline out of a soap opera," says Jaynie, "but it hurt like hell all the same."

At the time, leaving seemed like a wise decision, especially from an emotional perspective. But it turned out to be an enormously costly one for Jaynie.

Like many women of her fortysomething generation, she had married young, supported her husband through law school, and happily went from rags to riches along with him as his career blossomed while she took care of home and hearth. Little did Jaynie know that it would be back to square one after the divorce.

"I was at an incredible disadvantage right from the beginning," Jaynie recalls. "There wasn't a divorce attorney worth his salt who would represent me. My husband was Crown Prince of the old boys' network of lawyers in L.A., and no one would touch me with a ten-foot pole." So Jaynie decided to use mediation, hoping to come to a speedy and amicable agreement with her husband. Big mistake.

The mediation team included an attorney and a psychologist. But what Jaynie really needed was a top-notch accountant to sort through some very thorny financial issues. "I actually did hire someone, but my husband said that she made him nervous, so I got rid of her. I don't know what I was thinking," she says now, still shaking her head in disbelief. Things went rapidly downhill from there.

"*Everything* became an issue, and it got to a point where I had just about had enough. I couldn't bring myself to get down in the dirt and roll around with him anymore," Jaynie says with a sigh. "But I have to say that the last straw was his showing up at my daughter's birthday party with his twenty-five-year-old secretary on his arm. That's when I decided to pick up my marbles and leave."

Unfortunately for Jaynie, she was so determined to get out of Dodge that she didn't even take the time to read her final settlement agreement. The mediator had drawn up a proposal that Jaynie and her husband had both agreed to, but her husband had insisted on retyping it—"Just to incorporate some language changes," he said. The language changes—which Jaynie didn't notice in her haste to sign on the dotted line—turned out to be a lot more substantive than just crossing some t's and dotting some i's. They were so extensive, in fact, that today, nearly eight years after her divorce, Jaynie can still barely make ends meet.

"Every day is a struggle," she says, "and on my worst days, it's a financial nightmare."

Never do money and emotions more painfully intersect than during and immediately following a divorce. At no other time are a woman's net worth and her self-worth so completely intertwined. During divorce negotiations money becomes a symbol of all that has gone wrong in the marriage. Pain, anger, jealousy, and guilt all culminate in arguments about money.

The emotional and financial dynamics of divorce are unlike those of any other life transition. The fears, uncertainties, and self-doubts that plague every divorcing woman, if not recognized and dealt with, will inevitably prevent her from making critical financial decisions in her own best interest—especially during the all-important negotiation stage.

That charming stereotype of the Cruella de Ville ex-wife trying to bleed her poor husband dry surfaces every time a woman insists on getting what she deserves. And, sadly, women often sabotage their own financial interests just to prove that they don't fit the stereotype.

Do you think an ex-husband appreciates what his wife sacrifices by not going after the money she deserves? Does he thank her for making their divorce so amicable? Or does he pat himself on the back for making his own shrewd business deal? I wonder . . .

Over the past several years I have had the privilege of speaking to tens of thousands of women all across the country. One particular speech stands out in my mind because it affected me so deeply, so viscerally. I was speaking to a group of divorced and divorcing women, and their questions absolutely floored me:

> I'd like to keep my house, but I don't know if I can afford to live there. My kids don't want to change schools, and they're already blaming me for the divorce even though my husband was the one who left. Should I keep the house or uproot my kids?

> I don't know where to go for help. After our divorce, my husband got the CPA, the banker, and the stockbroker. I got four boxes full of paperwork I don't understand, and there is no one to explain it to me. I don't even know who to ask. I feel like such a zero.

What do I do when my husband threatens to take away my kids unless I agree to his financial terms? I'm scared to death of losing my children even though I know what he's doing is totally unfair.

Divorce *isn't* fair.

And the cost of divorce is incredibly high, in both financial and psychological terms.

From 1950 to 1990 the number of divorces in the United States more than tripled. Today, there are more than thirteen million divorced men and women in America.[1] But life after divorce is by no means a level playing field. Consider the following figures:

• **The ratio of divorced women's mean earnings to those of their ex-husbands is less than half.[2]**

• **Only 15 percent of all divorcing women receive any form of *spousal support* whatsoever.[3]**

• **Of the women who *are* awarded *alimony* payments, more than 25 percent never receive a penny of them.[4]**

• **More than a million children under age eighteen live in divorced households, the overwhelming majority with their mothers.[5]**

• **Only 48 percent of women who are awarded child support receive the full amount to which they are entitled. Twenty-five percent receive no child support at all.[6]**

Over one million marriages will end in divorce this year. Over one million women will *not* live happily ever after. They will, even by conservative estimates, suffer a 24 percent decrease in living standards, while their ex-husbands' fortunes will drop by 5 percent at most.[7] They will wonder what they could have done differently to make their marriages work, while their ex-husbands join health clubs and start going out on dates.

Take the case of Marla and Rob: Marla, fifty-two, contin-

Note: The terms *alimony* and *spousal support* are used interchangeably throughout.

ued to torture herself for months after her divorce, asking over and over again what she had done wrong, believing that she had somehow driven her husband away. She never should have started working, she thought. Things were fine until she took that teaching job two years ago. That must have been it. Rob must have felt emasculated, as if she were telling the world that he couldn't provide a good enough living for her, that he couldn't take care of her.

Marla berated herself endlessly, agonizing over how she could have behaved differently and perhaps stayed married.

Reality check: While Marla was busy blaming herself, Rob was busy moving in with his new girlfriend. He was also busy joining a fitness center and buying a collection of Kenny G tapes and a cappuccino machine to go along with them.

What's wrong with this picture?

It's been said that "women mourn, men replace." In my extensive work with divorced and divorcing women, I've seen it over and over again: Men going through a divorce lose twenty pounds and buy a red car; women going through a divorce look like they've been through the spin cycle on their washing machine. My conclusion: Divorce hurts. But it hurts women a lot more than men.

Especially from a financial perspective.

Never in life are money and emotions so inextricably bound as they are during and after a divorce. Money becomes a reward for whoever succeeds at the emotional bartering game. But the emotional wear and tear of divorce often prevents women from making moneysmart decisions that will affect the rest of their lives.

Many divorcing women suffer from an overdeveloped sense of fair play that invariably creates unrealistic expectations for the outcome of settlement negotiations. "I assumed that when our marriage ended, my husband would want me to be financially secure. We're still friends. We don't hate each other. And, after all, it's only fair."

But "fair" doesn't even enter into it most of the time. Money and power do. Every argument, every issue, every bargaining point is about money—who earns it and who controls it. And during the months of divorce proceedings, many women are shocked to find that their husbands aren't interested in playing fair at all. No matter how long the marriage lasted or how amicable the split-up, once the divorce is under way, all previous bets are off.

Many women describe their husbands becoming abusive and secretive. Some husbands clean out joint checking and savings accounts behind their wives' backs, leaving them scraping the bottom of the financial barrel from the first moment that the divorce papers are filed. And some women are especially shocked to find out that their husbands have been planning the divorce for quite a long time, busily liquidating and hiding assets while they stood idly—and cluelessly—by. Discovering that their husbands have been sneaking behind their backs before they even suspected anything was wrong understandably leaves women feeling angry, hurt, and betrayed.

Deliberately or not, women *are* financially hurt after divorce. This is especially true of women over forty who have not worked extensively outside the home. If you're a fortysomething plus woman, chances are that you have devoted considerable time to raising your family and taking care of home and hearth so your husband could focus on his career. Faced with divorce, no matter what settlement you ultimately receive, your husband will leave the marriage with his job, his work skills, and an education that you may have helped pay for when you were first married. You, on the other hand, may be leaving the marriage with none of the above. There is no way your settlement can make up for this.

Divorce is a process of redefining fairness to include being fair to yourself first and foremost.

Since time immemorial, women have been instilled with the belief that Prince Charming is out there somewhere, waiting to spirit us away on his snow-white horse. We're taught that if we're good, we can expect to live happily ever after. But hanging your long ponytail out the window of a tower like a latter-day Rapunzel waiting to be rescued just doesn't work in real life.

Women need to learn how to rescue themselves.

Every emotional step that a woman takes during the divorce process is linked to independence: independence from a relationship, from the concept of a two-parent family, from an ideal of how life *should* be. And each stride that a woman takes away from her old life brings her one step closer to her new life.

In this new life, money will play a different, much more important, role than it once did. So if it's hard to say good-bye to the white knight ideal of a husband who would protect you and take care of you forever, it may be even harder to say hello to your new role as independent manager of your own money. Hard, but not impossible—and *not* optional.

Divorce is more than just desensitized number crunching. It's more than dividing up tables and chairs and bank accounts. It's walking into the restaurant where you celebrated your last anniversary and feeling your knees buckle under you. It's seeing your ex-husband and his perky little girlfriend come to pick up your kids, and suddenly feeling a wave of nausea so strong that half the bank account doesn't make you feel any better—at least not at that moment. Divorce is about emotions all mixed up with money all mixed up with more emotions.

"Doing money" may not come naturally to many women. In fact, it might seem downright terrifying. But it *can* be done. Whatever the size or nature of your settlement, there is a financial strategy that will make the most of your money. Whether you need to pay off debts immediately or plan for your retirement twenty years down the road, the time to start being moneysmart is now.

This book contains step-by-step guidelines to help you separate your emotions from your money and actively participate in negotiating a moneysmart divorce. Because divorce is a multistage process, the book is divided into five sections, reflecting the five different stages of the divorce process.

In the *Decision* stage, you may be painfully aware of the fact that your marriage isn't working but unsure about whether it's really over. This is a time when you and your husband may fight openly, go for counseling, seek legal representation, and physically separate. Does this mean that you will, in fact, divorce? Should you prepare for divorce if it's not a certainty? Some couples do get back together after "pre-divorce," but most don't.

Once the decision to divorce has been made, you'll begin building an "A team" of experts who will help guide you through the bewildering maze of the divorce process and its aftermath. This can be an emotionally devastating time, regardless of who initiated the split. How will you make the transition from being a couple to being a single? How will your family and friends react? What will you tell your children?

By learning what questions to ask, which documents to gather, and how to take other important financial fact-finding steps, you'll begin the process of becoming financially independent and learning how to stand on your own two feet.

The *Planning Period* can be an extremely volatile time, characterized by anger, feelings of betrayal, and fear of loneliness. At this point you'll start evaluating your assets, documenting your expenses, figuring out how family bills will be paid during your separation, and negotiating for temporary spousal and child support. You'll also become all too familiar with the legalese of discovery, depositions, interrogatories, and subpoenas. And, if need be, you will learn how to ferret out hidden assets and how to protect yourself from divorce dirty tricks.

By the time you've reached the *Big Picture* stage, you'll have come to terms with the fact that the divorce is real and inevitable. The decision to divorce has been made, and your plans for moving forward are well under way. The initial trauma has passed, and you're doing okay—perhaps even better than you expected.

Now is when taking a good hard look at the Big Picture helps you get a handle on your homeowner's expenses, your business, your retirement plan, your taxes, and every other nuance of your financial life—past, present, and future. As a result, you're well prepared to discuss settlement strategies, divide up your assets and liabilities, and make important financial decisions involving alimony and child support.

Then comes the period of *Resolution* when you truly make the transition from two to one. But just when you think you see the light at the end of the tunnel, you may find yourself going into aftershock. The divorce becomes final in this stage, and the emotional and financial reality sets in, often with a huge jolt to your psyche *and* to your pocketbook. During this time you may feel an overwhelming sense of failure and low self-esteem. The feeling is normal, and it will pass.

As you hammer out the final terms of your settlement and complete the legal and financial business of your divorce, you begin looking forward as you plan for your financial future.

In the final, *Reentry* stage of your divorce, you'll begin to live your life as a single woman and, perhaps, as a single parent. The divorce is over. You've lived to tell about it. The pain, the anger, and the resentment haven't vanished overnight, but you're starting to let go of these negative emotions. And you're starting to accept responsibility for your own emotional and financial well-being.

You'll continue working with your "A team" as you make financial decisions for yourself and your children, and you may enter or reenter the workplace as you adapt to your post-divorce budget, which may be considerably leaner than it was during your marriage.

The financial face of divorce has changed in recent years. It used to be that divorce settlements were based on who was at fault, and a cheating husband was considered grounds for high alimony payments. But today, most divorces in this country are "no fault," so the fight has shifted from fault to finance. Now, the mutual desire to end a relationship does not take into account who may have been "at fault" in the unhappy marriage. It doesn't matter. No-fault divorce treats assets and debts as common property and divides them between husband and wife. Earning power cannot be divided equally, however, which leaves women at a distinct disadvantage. Many older women have never worked outside the home, and many younger women still earn far less than their male counterparts for doing the same job. Unfortunately, this disparity rarely gets worked into the settlement agreement. Again, fair doesn't enter into it.

The face of the divorced woman has also changed in recent years. Although the average divorcee is a thirtysomething woman who has been married approximately seven years, divorce has bridged the generation gap with more women in their forties and fifties divorcing this year than ever before.

And contrary to public opinion, not all divorced women over the age of forty get left by their husbands. Many initiate the divorce or do the leaving themselves. This doesn't make them any less vulnerable to emotional blackmail, however. Often, these women feel so much guilt for "destroying" the marriage, not to mention the family, that they settle for far less money than they deserve when it comes time to negotiate a financial arrangement.

Not all children of divorce are young children anymore, either. They are often adult children well into their twenties or thirties. Traditionally, child support payments stop cold when the kids turn eighteen. But the reality is that in today's economy, most eighteen-year-olds are light-years away from being financially independent. If they plan to go to college, who pays? And if the adult children need to move back home while they're getting their post-college careers off the ground, is Mom's settlement supposed to support them, too?

No matter how many kids you have, how much money you

have, how old you are, or how long you've been married, you have something in common with every other woman reading this book right now. For them, like you, divorce signals the end of a relationship that is an integral part of nearly every woman's life—and so much a part of her self-definition.

Elaine vividly recalls the day when, newly divorced with both children away at college, she found herself walking up and down the aisles of the supermarket wondering, "What does Elaine like to eat?" Not "What does Jerry like?" or "What do the kids like?" but "What does *Elaine* like?"

She had always shopped for a family of four and honestly didn't know what to buy for herself. Overwhelmed by her suddenly single status and her newfound "freedom," Elaine left her cart in the middle of the supermarket aisle and headed for home. "How will I ever get used to the idea of making decisions for myself if I can't even decide between bagels and English muffins?" she thought.

It was scary, intimidating. But it was also her first real chance to get to know herself. Married during her sophomore year in college and a mother twice over at age twenty-one, Elaine had never had that opportunity before. Her divorce gave her the chance to finally discover who Elaine is—and what Elaine likes to eat!

Without question, going through a divorce is a traumatic experience. But it is *not* a life-threatening one. Many women like Elaine do move beyond the confusion and the emotional turmoil only to discover a much better life after divorce.

The divorce process is a painful one, but it also—ultimately—can be a positive one. While much is lost, much can be gained, particularly in terms of financial awareness and independence.

Divorce Myths and Realities

Misconceptions abound concerning the financial realities of divorce. Being moneysmart means separating fact from fiction. Consider the following divorce myths and realities:

Myth: Even after your divorce, alimony payments will support you in the style to which you're accustomed.
Reality: Don't bet on it! In the state of California, only one out of every six women receives any form of spousal support whatsoever. Nationwide, the number drops to about one in seven.

Myth: Older women generally fare much better financially than younger women after a divorce.
Reality: The median income of older divorced women (age sixty-two and older) is a paltry $9,000 per year and has been growing at a below-inflation rate of 1.5 percent.[8]

Myth: You may not be able to depend on spousal support, but if you're a mom, you can certainly count on receiving child support.
Reality: Guess again. According to a White House task force on welfare reform, only $13 billion is collected in child support each year versus $47 billion that is actually owed.

Myth: Don't worry if your husband threatens to sue for child custody. Most judges still feel that children should be with their mothers.
Reality: True, but that's changing. In the 1970s, only 1 percent of divorcing fathers were awarded custody of their children. Today, that number is 20 percent to 25 percent.[9]

Myth: You're better off going to court than haggling over every nickel and dime with your ex.

Reality: In most cases, you'll get a better deal by *not* going to court. A settlement agreement between you and your ex can be tailored to your specific needs. The courts will divide everything up without regard to consequences.

Myth: If you hang in there long enough, you'll end up with a divorce settlement that's fair and just.

Reality: Maybe. Persistence certainly helps. But if your ex is determined to fight you at every turn and he's even prepared to face contempt charges or jail, there's not much you can do. You may grow old waiting for justice to be served.

Myth: Using the same divorce lawyer as your husband will save you time, money, and a lot of grief.

Reality: Don't even think about it. It's an accident waiting to happen! You need to be sure that your lawyer is working for *you* alone and is protecting *your* best interests.

I gain strength, courage, and confidence by every experience in
   which I must stop and look fear in the face. . . .
I say to myself, I've lived through this and can take the next
   thing that comes along. . . .
We must do the things we think we cannot do.
                                          —*Eleanor Roosevelt*

It's amazing how healing money can be.
                                          —*Dolly Parton*

PART I

· · ·

Making the Divorce Decision

Hope Springs Eternal

●●●

Judy and Daniel had been separated for eleven months. They tried marriage counseling but were not able to work through the differences that had wedged a big question mark in the future of their eighteen-year marriage. But even after almost a year apart, Judy still had hope. She and Daniel had merely separated, she reasoned, and if he would only make more of an effort in their sessions with the marriage counselor, they could surely reconcile. They just needed time to sort things out. There was no reason to think about splitting up the bank account because they weren't really going to get divorced. Her parents hadn't raised her to cut and run out of a marriage that wasn't working. Divorce was something that most emphatically would *not* happen in her life.

Too bad Daniel wasn't on the same page of that particular storybook. He was already seeing someone new, and, in fact, they were practically living together. He wasn't making any kind of effort to reconcile with Judy. He sat through their counseling sessions in stony silence while she poured her heart out.

One thing was clear: Judy was in denial. Big time. Their life together might have looked prettier that way, but it wasn't vaguely realistic. She was ignoring the red flag that Daniel was waving right before her eyes. The fate of her marriage had been sealed long before Daniel moved out of their home. Months later, when Daniel moved again—this time out of his condo and in with his girlfriend—Judy could no longer convince even herself that they would get back together. It was only then that she filed for divorce.

Like Judy, women often embrace marriage like a warm puppy, while men are already moving on to the next stage in their lives. In my opinion, it makes good sense to consider at least the possibility of divorce if you find yourself in a similar situation. Of course, reconciliation *is* a possibility for some couples. Just because you've separated doesn't mean that the marriage is necessarily over. But separation should be a time for assessing the what-if's. What if counseling doesn't work? What if my husband doesn't want to reconcile even if I do? What if he wants to get back together and I don't? What if my marriage *is* over?

Judy wasn't ready to ask—or answer—these questions at first. "I didn't want to jinx any possibility of a reconciliation," she says. You may feel the same way: afraid that if you say the word "divorce" out loud, your fate will be etched in stone and your life will be changed forever. Judy recalls sitting for hours, paralyzed with fear, trying to face a notepad filled with names of divorce attorneys recommended to her by friends. "Just make an appointment," they'd tell her. Over and over again, her hand reached for the telephone, and each time something pulled her back. If she saw a lawyer, would she be sealing the fate of her marriage? Of course not. That was like thinking that by buying fire insurance she was dooming her house to burn to the ground. But to Judy, that's exactly how it felt.

Somehow, admitting that divorce might happen seems like it would bring it one step closer to happening. And you may be afraid that if your husband finds out that you've taken steps to prepare for the possibility, there will be almost no chance of reconciliation. It's easier to close your eyes, think back to your wedding day, and convince yourself that ignorance is bliss. Yet if you really believed that, you wouldn't be reading this book in the first place, would you? Even though it's tough to admit, divorce may be the only way to move to a happier place in your life.

The Decision stage is about getting in touch with, and in control of, what comes next—whatever comes next. What you will learn by going through the process of "Making the Divorce Decision" is how to take control of your financial life within your marriage or without it. Even in the happiest marriage, there is still plenty of room to get a better handle on your joint finances. And it's always better to be safe than sorry.

When Your Heart Falls in the Cuisinart

The Decision stage takes a toll on your emotions, often an unbearably heavy toll. In one fell swoop you go from the security of a marriage (albeit one that isn't working) to the insecurity of the unknown. Getting through this stage takes a massive dose of positive reinforcement. You have to remind yourself constantly that you can get through this. You know you can. If you do make the decision to divorce, at times you may seriously doubt your ability to survive, and you may feel like going back to what was—no matter how bad it was. As unhappy as you might have been in your marriage, you think it must have been better than what you're going through now. But was it really? Going through a divorce hurts, but staying in a bad marriage hurts much more.

Clearly, your relationship with your husband is *not* what it once was. Not by a long shot. Dissatisfaction may have turned into fighting, fighting may have turned into open warfare. Some couples get to the point, even in this early stage, where they can barely be civil to each other. If you're still friendly and on good terms, count your lucky stars. Many women aren't as fortunate.

If you decide to initiate a breakup, you may find yourself second-guessing your decision. Yesterday, it was the right thing to do. Today, it seems shortsighted and hasty. Tomorrow, who knows? You're on an emotional roller coaster going up, down, and sideways.

Many women blame themselves for the fact that the marriage isn't working, going over and over in their minds the ways they can try to "save" the marriage. If you decide that you really have tried everything and it really is time to end the marriage, you still may be worried that your children will blame you and that your parents will be disappointed and will accuse you of not sticking it out through the rough times.

You may feel despair and the overwhelming sense that, like Humpty Dumpty, you'll never be able to put the pieces of your life back together again. These are common and perfectly legitimate feelings. If you're not experiencing them now, chances are that you will feel this way at some point if you proceed with the divorce. But the good news is that there *is* life after divorce, and you're already taking the first steps toward getting there—sometimes after much hesitation and with great regret.

"I know it's time to call it quits," laments thirty-seven-year-old Jamie, a senior creative director at a San Francisco–based advertising agency, "but I can't believe it's really over. And I can't believe how antagonistic he's become. I remember when Andrew and I first started dating twelve years ago. He really, truly swept me off my feet, and I'm scared to death that I'll never feel that way about another man again," she says. "Even now, that frightened little voice inside my head tells me to just stay with Andrew."

One of the most difficult aspects of accepting even the possibility of divorce is dealing with the intense pain of rejecting or being rejected. You may have spent months or years being married and miserable, but the thought that it's really over can make you want to rewrite history. Suddenly, your husband's flaws aren't so terrible and the fighting isn't so awful.

The idea of living alone—physically, emotionally, and financially alone—may terrify you, even if you're a take-charge twentysomething businesswoman with your own financial resources. And especially if you're a forty-five-year-old homemaker who depends on her husband to bring home the bacon and balance the books.

It's easy to let your fears get the better of your common sense. And when they do, your husband with all his flaws takes on the newly polished shining armor of a gallant knight on a white horse. He can comfort you. He can take care of you. He can sweep away all the scary thoughts of being out there, alone and vulnerable. This is a man who can rescue you. He can save you from the twin dragons of fear and loneliness, and give you back the idyllic life that you had before. (Okay, even if it wasn't so idyllic.)

In this scenario, he has all the power and you have none. Even in your fantasy, someone else controls your destiny. Isn't that even scarier than being alone? But in reality, you're *not* alone. And now—when you may be having second and even third thoughts about your divorce—it's especially important to realize that you're not alone.

Whether you're 90 percent determined to go forward with the divorce or vacillating daily—or even hourly—between "Should I?" and "Shouldn't I?" don't try to go it alone. Get professional help. Make an appointment with a therapist if you're not seeing one already, and by all means call a lawyer if only for a preliminary consultation to examine your options.

Overcoming Emotional Paralysis: Making the First Phone Call

Somehow picking up the phone and calling an attorney may seem akin in your mind to picking up a kitchen knife and cutting the heart right out of your marriage. You don't want to take that step. You just don't want to make that call. It's one thing to think about getting divorced; it's quite another thing actually to get on the phone to a lawyer.

Remember, though, that you're calling for a consultation. *Only* a consultation. Your first visit to a lawyer will not set in motion anything permanent or irreversible. In fact, if you feel like you're being talked into doing something that you're not comfortable with, voice your feelings, trust your instincts, and, if necessary, get up and leave. Choosing a lawyer has little to do with listening to your next-door neighbor's advice, and everything to do with listening to your own warm fuzzies—your strong, intuitive feelings of comfort—and good common sense.

Be sure to consider all your options. Hiring an attorney is only one of several alternatives that you can explore. In the Decision stage, you should consider non-attorney options as well. And just as making a preliminary appointment to talk with an attorney doesn't seal the fate of your marriage, it also doesn't necessarily mean that you will even use that attorney should you decide to proceed with your divorce.

The Initial Consultation: Questions to Ask

It's important to let your prospective lawyer know right from the start that you're planning to take an active role in getting a moneysmart divorce should it come to that. And be sure to make it clear from the get-go that if you do proceed with the divorce, you want to be kept up to date on everything that happens in your case. Ask for a complete explanation of your legal rights—in English, not in legalese—and make sure that you understand everything that's being explained to you. If you don't, keep asking questions until you understand *all* the answers.

If you're not exactly sure what to ask during your initial legal consultation, here are some questions that will help you get straight to the bottom line on costs, procedures, time frame, and reasonable expectations for the process of divorce:

1. **How much will this cost me?** Some attorneys offer a free one-hour initial consultation; others, however, charge their hourly billing rate right from the get-go, which can range from $100 to $500 or more.

Your lawyer won't be able to tell you at the outset exactly how much your divorce will cost, but you may be able to get a pretty good estimate based on the assets involved, the possibility of custody issues being raised, and the degree of agreement or acrimony between the divorcing parties. Find out about hourly rates and evening or weekend rates. Also, ask if the lawyer will expect a bonus tied to the amount of the final settlement. Some do, some don't. Attorneys are often required by law to have you sign a written retainer agreement. Find out how much the retainer fee will be, when it must be paid, and if it is refundable in the event that you do not go forward with the divorce. In some cases, it is. (The retainer is a lump sum that is paid up front from which subsequent fees are deducted.) And don't forget to find out what other costs you may incur—photocopying, faxing, messenger service, and so forth—and when these bills are due and payable. Finally, ask if your lawyer will try to get your husband to pay a portion of your retainer and additional legal fees as part of the settlement agreement.

2. **What are the *specifics* of the retainer agreement?** The retainer should spell out in advance exactly what expenses you can expect. If there are different hourly rates for evenings or weekends, your retainer should state this. And if you want to be consulted before evening or weekend hours are spent on your case, this is the time to put that in writing. Costs for mailing and travel or meal expenses should also be outlined. Again, if you want to be consulted before agreed-upon maximums are exceeded, include that provision in the written agreement now.

3. **How long will my divorce take?** Maybe your lawyer can't give you specifics, but you *can* get an estimate of the time frame required to finalize your divorce. This will depend on

factors such as the complexity of the issues under discussion, the assets to be divided, and, of course, how soon you and your ex-to-be can stop arguing and start negotiating an agreement. You should certainly know if you're looking at six months or two years. It helps to know that it's a finite period of time and not the never-ending story. And it also helps you figure out how much money you need to live on during the proceedings. (More about this in Part II.)

4. **What can you tell me about your firm?** Other than the firm's size, you'll also want to know whether the firm specializes in matrimonial law. If not, what percentage of its client work involves divorce cases? Ask specifically about past cases—how many were settled out of court and how many went to trial? In most cases, the optimal goal is to settle out of court. If you do end up in court, the judge may add up your assets, divide everything as he deems appropriate, and end your chances of negotiating a more favorable settlement. Be wary of a law firm that doesn't have a good track record for settling most cases out of court.

5. **Who will be working on my case?** The larger the firm, the greater the likelihood that there will be people other than your attorney working on your case. Find out who these people are and whether there are substantially lower billing rates when more junior lawyers, paralegals, or secretaries are doing the work. This could save you a lot of money in the long run. It isn't a drawback to have other people working on your case as long as they are properly supervised by your attorney and are fully qualified to perform the tasks assigned to them. You do, however, want your attorney to handle any settlement negotiations personally and to go to court on your behalf, if necessary. If you choose a small firm, make sure your lawyer has the time and resources to handle your case. Find out about the time commitment your case will require and whether your lawyer has other commitments that might cause your case to take longer than necessary. Even the best lawyers can get overloaded at times.

Going the Lawyer Route

If you've been married for a long time or have extensive pension funds, joint assets, trust accounts, and so forth, you'll likely need an attorney to sort through everything for you and help negotiate the best possible settlement. If so, consider consulting at least two to three lawyers in order to find the one with whom you can develop the best working relationship.

Personal referrals can be an excellent way to narrow down your search to the handful of lawyers whom you want to interview. Your estate, tax, or business attorney may also be able to refer you to a colleague who specializes in family law. (Just be sure that your husband isn't consulting the same attorney for referrals.) Recently divorced friends who had a good experience with their lawyers are also good bets for qualified recommendations.

You may also want to take a look at the national register of lawyers for a comprehensive list of attorneys in your area. And if you like, you can even visit your local library and look for newspaper and magazine articles referencing different law firms and lawyers who specialize in divorce. But before you proceed further, check with your city and state attorney's office to make sure that there are no complaints on file against these lawyers or law firms.

Accept No Less Than You Deserve

If you select an attorney and decide to go forward with your divorce, you should expect to be kept up to date on all negotiations with your husband's lawyer. This includes receiving copies of any letters or other communications between your lawyer and your husband's lawyer. Again, don't be afraid to ask for English-language translations of confusing legalese. It's hard to know what you're signing when you don't understand what the words mean. If you aren't well versed in legal jargon—and most of us certainly aren't—ask for a clear explanation, and, of course, don't sign or agree to anything until you get it.

If you need to, also ask for a clear explanation of your attorney's bills. The invoices that you receive should detail all expenses including telephone time, research hours, travel time, photocopying, faxing, and office visits. Get used to what the bills look like so you'll notice immediately if one month seems unusual or if the expenses seem out of whack. If there's a mysterious charge, question it. It could just be a case of an unfamiliar billing abbreviation, but it could also be a mistake.

Remember, when dealing with your attorney, you will be charged by the hour or even in increments as small as six minutes, whether you spend that time evaluating your financial needs or venting your frustration at your husband's indifference to your feelings. Venting is fine if you need to vent. Your feelings are important and more than appropriate. But unless you've got big bucks to burn, paying a lawyer $250 to $500 an hour to listen to them isn't appropriate. You may not be able to avoid waves of anger or tears of frustration from time to time, but on an ongoing basis, you'll be infinitely better off talking about your feelings with a qualified therapist than with your attorney—and it will certainly cost you a lot less.

It's best to try to keep your valuable attorney minutes focused on your case and on strictly legal issues. It also helps to do your homework: Make lists of questions that you want to ask and stay focused on the financial goals that you want to achieve in your settlement. You can take notes during your attorney meetings and review what you discussed when you get home. You can even bring a small tape recorder along with you if you like. Always do whatever works best for you.

A final note on establishing a good working relationship with your attorney: If you have decided to go forward with your divorce, you've already made the commitment to get out of a bad marriage. Likewise, if your attorney relationship isn't off to a good start and doesn't show signs of improving, think seriously about ending it now. There can be a tendency to stay with an attorney you don't feel comfortable with—or even like—just to prove to yourself that you can make *this* relationship work. Don't make an emotional investment here. This is one tie that you can easily sever with no real repercussions except perhaps for a little wasted time and money. Better to cut your losses now than risk staying in *any* relationship where you're not getting what you want or what you deserve.

Keeping Legal Costs Down

Once you have found a lawyer whom you can work with, remember to be moneysmart even in your dealings with your attorney.

The best thing you can do to avoid unnecessary legal expenses is *be prepared*. It's tempting to dump a pile of papers in your attorney's lap with instructions to wake you when it's all over. Resist the urge. The more you know about your case and the more you can do yourself, the less money you'll spend on fees and the better the settlement you're likely to get.

Remember, even a ten-minute phone conversation with your attorney will cost you money. "I once asked my attorney at what point he actually starts billing me during a telephone conversation," recounts Lisa. "Can you believe that the meter starts running right after he says, 'Hi, how are you?'!" Sad, but true. Even if you call only to ask one question, you may be billed a minimum amount. So try to save your questions for your next face-to-face meeting or at least for a longer phone call when you have a whole list of things to ask.

Be sure to keep a personal log of all telephone calls that you make to your lawyer, along with a note regarding what was discussed. Check it against your monthly bills to be certain that the numbers agree.

The very best way to keep costs down is to do as much as possible yourself. Any homework you can do to help locate and place a value on family assets saves your lawyer time and saves you money. You can also save money by helping with any research that has to be undertaken by accountants or private investigators, or even writing some of the letters to your husband and his attorney detailing the terms you'll agree to and the sticking points where you won't budge. Be sure, though, to have your lawyer look over all correspondence before it goes out.

Ask your lawyer what else you can do to help—and do it. Taking charge of at least part of your divorce proceedings will not only save you money but will also give you a feeling of personal empowerment that will serve you exceedingly well in your new life as an independent woman.

The Non-Attorney Options

If your divorce is not a complicated one, you can save money with one of the following options. A "do-it-yourself" divorce may be adequate for your situation.

• **100 Percent Do It Yourself.** The 100 percent do-it-yourself method works best when you have few assets and almost no debts. If you have been married a short time and your finances can be easily untangled, you can avoid high legal costs by obtaining the appropriate form from your local court. But if you have to figure in child support or if you begin arguing over each issue or asset, this method isn't for you. You'll be better off hiring someone to negotiate on your behalf.

• **Legal Clinic.** You should consider a legal clinic if your finances are relatively uncomplicated—if you've been married a short time, have no children, and have few assets to divide. Legal clinics can offer you the services of trained paralegals who are familiar with family law. And some legal clinics have full-fledged attorneys on staff who may be available for consultation for a limited amount of time. Legal clinics also take responsibility for filing all forms and paperwork with the court. Typical fees start at about $200 to $300 and can go appreciably higher depending on how complicated your divorce becomes.

If you have no money at all for legal assistance, you may still have the option, if it is available in your city, of seeking help from a community service legal clinic staffed entirely by volunteer attorneys and paralegals. Services may be limited and waiting time may be substantial. Check your local yellow pages for availability in your community.

• **Mediation** (also known as Alternative Dispute Resolution). This process differs from state to state, but it essentially requires hiring a go-between who can help you and your husband arrive at a workable compromise on issues where you disagree. A lawyer or judge can serve as a mediator, but be sure to choose that person very carefully. You obviously don't want someone who is biased in favor of your husband. Ask for references and check them thoroughly before agreeing on a mediator. You need to be certain your mediator has extensive knowledge of divorce law and clearly understands the financial ramifications of likely discussion points. A mediator is either "value added" or not—and if not, there's no point in having one.

Mediation works only if you know the value of your assets *and* you know how to locate them. Successful mediation depends on you and your husband bringing accurate information to the table. A mediator isn't going to hunt for hidden assets, so if you suspect that there's more to your joint finances than meets the eye, hire someone who can find out for sure.

There are cases, of course, when hiring even the best mediator in the world won't help. If your husband dominates the discussions and rolls his eyes every time you open your mouth or if you're being overtly bullied or coerced, a mediator isn't going to be a very effective go-between. You'll want to hire an attorney to represent you ASAP—someone who can push back when your husband keeps pushing your buttons over and over again.

• • •

In addition to your legal representation, you'll soon be in the company of people you can rely on to help you through your divorce—your own custom-built "A team" of advisers.

Your Divorce "A Team"

It's hard enough to get used to the new concept of personal and financial autonomy without feeling isolated from the rest of the world, too. It's also hard not to get so confused sometimes that you begin to feel isolated from your own instincts—what I call your "warm fuzzies." Warm fuzzies are not tangible. Often they're not even explainable. They're the feeling you get when you've made a decision that feels comfortable for you, that feels right to you. Warm fuzzies are strong intuitive feelings that should be respected, and never ignored.

When you're putting together your "A team" of professionals who will guide you through your divorce proceedings, think of your warm fuzzies as key players. Trust your instincts at all times when you're deciding which attorney to hire or whether to use Accountant A or Accountant B. Your warm fuzzies will come into play throughout your divorce and throughout your life after divorce as you continue to make personal and financial decisions on your own. Don't just rely on someone else's judgment. Look to yourself first to decide whether something *feels* right to you.

Your "A team" is made up of professionals whose job it is to help you make moneysmart divorce decisions. You'll rely on their knowledge and expertise when you have questions, and they'll keep you abreast of any new developments that can affect your divorce. But if for any reason your warm fuzzies warn you that a certain "A team" member isn't working out, *listen up!* Ignore your own instincts at your own peril.

You can custom-design your "A team" to fit your specific needs. You may very well want all new players on your team—professionals who don't have any connection to your married life. This is especially true if you believe that their loyalty may be to your husband instead of to you. But there are no hard-and-fast rules here. If you have a CPA whom you like and trust, there's nothing wrong with sticking with him. If it ain't broke, don't fix it. But you'd better fix it fast if your CPA informs you that he also plans to keep working for your husband. That doesn't work for you—and neither should he.

Your "A team" will include your divorce attorney, your accountant, and possibly a therapist. And do include friends and family on your team. Don't let misplaced embarrassment or stubborn pride stop you from reaching out for the help you need. Count on their support and accept it gladly and willingly.

Getting Your Ducks in a Row

The best way to save money is by remembering that the more you can do on your own, the less your attorney or accountant will have to do for you. During the Decision stage, your single most important task is to collect and make copies of any relevant paperwork, even the odds and ends that have found their way into a storage cabinet in your garage or a shoebox under your bed. Start looking immediately. Even if you're not sure whether a document is relevant to your divorce, make a copy of it just to be safe.

If you haven't finally and unequivocally made the decision to divorce, you may feel as though this is a waste of time at best and a violation of privacy at worst. Common sense dictates, though, that you're better off gathering the paperwork now rather than risk missing the opportunity altogether. If push comes to shove and the divorce goes forward, you'll be glad that you did what you had to do in spite of your reservations. The main purpose of gathering this paperwork is to document your joint income and assets and to illustrate the standard of living to which you are accustomed.

What types of documents should you be on the lookout for? Anything and everything even remotely connected to your household and family finances, including:

- **Tax returns from previous years.** Make two copies of your federal and state joint tax returns for the past five years. If you file separately, make copies of both sets of returns.
- **Receipts, bills, credit card statements, deeds, valuations, or other paperwork (including a do-it-yourself list) detailing and describing every asset you own—or at least everything that you can think of.** Take pictures as proof. This includes photographing the contents of any safety deposit boxes. List property you and your husband own separately and anything you own together. Don't forget to include your house, vacation home, or any other real estate holdings. You can generally stick to the big-ticket items, but if a particular possession means a great deal to you, include it on your list even if it is of minimal value. If it's important to you, it's important enough to list.
- **Bank statements; passbooks; checking, savings, and money market accounts; and CDs.**
- **A complete and detailed accounting of stocks, bonds, mutual funds, precious metals, annuities, limited partnerships, and any other financial instruments that either or both of you own.** Note the current market value of all securities and make copies of purchase confirmations to show what was bought, when, and at what price.
- **Retirement plans** including IRAs (yours and his) as well as 401(k)s, SEP-IRAs, Keoghs, and any company-sponsored pension plans. (More about retirement plans in Part III.)
- **Additional statements that fully describe your employee benefits as well as your husband's.**
- **All insurance policies,** including life, health, disability, homeowner's, renter's, or other coverage.

And Don't Overlook . . .

In your search through desk drawers and file cabinets, you're not just looking for old tax returns and department store receipts. You can significantly improve your chances of getting a settlement that reflects and maintains your current standard of living if you can document your lifestyle. There are several ways to do this:

1. **Illustrate your standard of living:** Nothing will better illustrate your lifestyle than solid documentation of your current living expenses. If you're used to going to the hairdresser once a week and maintaining a costly membership at a local country club, you'll want that to be factored into your settlement. If you're accustomed to living well, prove it.

In doing so, you can also help estimate your husband's income. So even if he has been consistently underreporting his income on his tax returns—and it's been known to happen—you can prove that he must be making more money than he claims he is and that you're entitled to a piece of that bigger pie. You can do this by documenting your living expenses—from what you spend on essentials like food and clothing to the luxuries you've become used to, like a Hawaiian vacation each winter and a new car every two years. The better you are at documenting your standard of living during your marriage, the better you'll be at negotiating a moneysmart settlement.

2. **Show your contribution to family income:** Collect old paycheck stubs and records of deposits that you made to personal and joint accounts.

If you contributed to your husband's business by balancing his books or even by helping him prepare presentations for out-of-town business trips, keep a record of this contribution. It counts.

If you helped your husband establish his career or start his own business by supporting the family while he was in school, don't forget to list this as a contribution. Likewise, if you put your education on hold to support him while he obtained an advanced degree that he's now using to make a living, count this as a contribution as well.

If you, your parents, or other family members lent your husband money to start his practice or business, or if you co-signed a bank loan for him, gather the documents that verify these actions.

3. **Demonstrate your contribution to the family-owned business:** Document your title and salary for any job that you held. Even if your title doesn't appear on tax forms or loan applications, it helps if you can show it on company brochures, letters addressed to you at your place of business, or company correspondence mailed out over your signature.

4. **Look for records of joint debts:** List all business, college, mortgage, consumer, or other debts that you carry jointly, including any purchases that you bought on credit while married. Also note when all loans are due and who must be paid.

Be sure to obtain a copy of your credit report, which may list debts that your husband has incurred without your even knowing it. Finding out the truth now can avoid a nasty surprise later on.

5. **Document childcare-related tasks and expenses:** Make a list of *everything* that you do for your children—whether it's driving them to school, shopping for their food or clothing, teaching them to play tennis, or arranging for tutors. Should you get into a custody battle down the road, you'll want to be able to document your role in their lives, particularly if you're the primary caregiver.

6. **If your husband was financially "at fault" in the marriage, gather proof:** Even in a no-fault divorce, financial fault may play a role. If you can document fault, for example, by proving that your husband squandered your family's money on vacations that he took with "someone else" or wasted money on needless purchases for that person, you may have considerable bargaining power.

You can be sure that forty-nine-year-old May who was struggling to get by on $300 a week during her marriage was shocked to find a receipt for a $250 gold bracelet in hubby Harold's jacket pocket. As May's attorney later discovered, the entire time Harold was pleading poverty to May, he was playing sugar daddy to his girlfriend, Rita. Uncovering the truth helped May negotiate a more favorable settlement and no doubt meant that Rita had to forgo a set of matching earrings.

In a no-fault divorce, infidelity may not be a sin but subsidizing it is another story altogether. You can also make a case for fault if you can prove that your husband intentionally gambled your money away or depleted joint funds on excessive living expenses during your separation.

Getting Down to Business

Truly, the best way to achieve a moneysmart divorce is to approach the process as if you were preparing for a business negotiation. That sounds ridiculous, right? You may feel more like you're prepping for an emotional prizefight, afraid your composure won't make it through the first round. But the more clearheaded and businesslike you can be, the better your chances of getting what you deserve. If you can't be emotionally detached—and some women can't—do try to be as financially objective as possible.

Let your attorney do his or her job. Be prepared for tough questions going in. At the beginning, they'll come from your lawyer; later on, from your husband's. Know what to expect in advance.

Getting down to the business of divorce even at this early stage means taking the following steps:

• **Apply for credit in your own name and keep careful track of your purchases so you don't end up in a massive credit crunch.** Obtaining credit is a good first step on the road to financial independence; going into debt isn't.

• **Keep a log of your expenses so you can get a feel for how** much you'll need to live on during your separation. If you haven't separated yet, pay any bills out of your joint account—in full if you can. But if you can't, you can't. For the moment, don't worry about paying off existing debts. Just don't create any new ones.

• **Maintain your standard of living, and don't start scrimping on daily necessities for fear of what will happen later on.** This doesn't mean splurging on unnecessary things, but it does mean living the way you're accustomed to living and giving your children what they need. If you need clothes, buy them using joint funds. Make sure that you have a wardrobe for the workplace. And if possible, take care of home repairs *before* separating.

• **Go to the doctor if you need to, and take your children to the doctor and dentist *before* separating.**

• **If you need to buy a car, try to do it before you separate.** Get a loan, arrange financing, and sign up for emergency roadside service. If your existing car needs repairs, have them taken care of now and pay for them out of your joint account.

• **Make note of any additional income that you receive, whether it's from Social Security payments, pension plans, investment interest, or other resources.** Write down where the money comes from, how often you receive it, and how much you count on per month.

• **Build up an emergency fund for legal fees and living expenses—optimally, six months' worth.**

• **Enroll in any career training courses you think you may need or sign up for academic classes.** If necessary, see a career counselor.

• **Keep all documents and financial records in one safe place, preferably in a locked drawer or cabinet.**

The Decision stage is obviously about much more than separating your financial interests from your husband's. It's also about physically separating, which is often the hardest part of all.

Home Sweet Home: Who Moves Out and When?

Home is where the heart is. A sad heart. In some cases, maybe a broken heart. As an investment professional, I tell a divorcing client to think of her house as an asset; as a living, caring human being, I tell her to think of it as her home, as an integral part of her past and, perhaps, her future.

Before you even begin thinking about whether you ultimately want to sell your house or keep it, you have to decide what to do with it during the separation period. Will you move out, or will he move out? And regardless of who goes where, how will the household expenses be paid? Who will take responsibility for getting the hedges trimmed and fixing the leaky plumbing, to say nothing of paying the mortgage and the property taxes?

It used to be a truism that when a couple split up, the husband automatically moved out. Not so anymore. These days it may be the wife who does the leaving. And in some cases, *no one* moves out—husband and wife continue living in the same house even after they're legally separated. This happens most often when one or both are attempting to establish "squatter's rights" that will influence the question of future ownership. But increasingly, divorcing couples who continue living together are doing so in the interest of their children still having Mom and Dad under one roof.

For most women, it's certainly a lot easier to keep living in the family home if only because you don't have to go anywhere physically. And, of course, if you stay in the house, you'll save your kids from being uprooted from school ties and neighborhood friends.

It's unlikely that you will be forced to sell the house at this time to raise cash quickly. Absent an immediate financial crisis, the path of least resistance may point you toward just living in the house because it's easier than dealing with real estate agents and having to hunt for a new place to live. Besides, it can make the divorce seem less brutal and less like an upheaval: You can keep living your life in the place you're accustomed to living it, with at least some sense of normalcy and familiarity.

"It was hard living in the house alone with the kids after Neil moved out three years ago," says Barbara, a twenty-nine-year-old stay-at-home mom with two young daughters. "But it was the right thing to do for all of us. This place is so perfect—a big old ranch house with lots of nooks and crannies where the kids can play hide-and-seek with all their friends in the neighborhood. The girls love the big backyard, too, and I know it would have been really hard for all of us to get used to a new place," she explains. "I don't like change. I like having everything right where it belongs, and the kids and I belong right where we are. Going through the divorce was hard enough without moving to a new place. I don't think I could have handled both at the same time."

Who Pays for What?

If your husband is planning to move out, be sure to determine *in advance* how the bills will be handled during the separation and who will be responsible for which expenses. He may share the costs of household upkeep with you, if only to protect his investment in this major asset so he can get maximum return when it's eventually sold. If you and your husband have decided to keep a joint account open to pay for other expenses during your separation, it might make sense to pay for household expenses out of this account as well.

On the other hand, some women take on the upkeep of the house without their husband's help. If you do so, you have every right to ask for a greater share of the proceeds when the house is sold if your settlement calls for the proceeds to be split after the sale.

If you stay in the house, you must manage it as an important financial asset. This means keeping up mortgage and insurance payments as well as property taxes. It also means keeping the house in good repair, the lawn properly cared for, and the trees trimmed so it doesn't look like a rundown nightmare if you decide to sell it and divide the proceeds as part of your settlement agreement. If you choose to take responsibility for upkeep of the family home, remember to keep track of your expenses so they can be taken into account when you're drafting your final settlement.

But I'd Rather Be the One Who Moves Out

The feeling of leaving can be liberating. If you pack up and walk out, *you're* the one who made the move. There's a sense of taking charge, of saying, "I didn't get left, *I* did the leaving." Besides, why would you want to live in a house where the two of you made all the memories—where you fought, made up, made love, made each other crazy?

There's no way my client Cynthia could have stayed in their condo after she and her husband Carl decided to split up after an eleven-year marriage. "I was out of there as fast as I could get my bags packed," she says. "Carl and I fought like cats and dogs for the last three years that we were together, so believe me, whatever fond memories I had of that place were long gone."

If you do decide to leave, go with the clear understanding that you may be irrevocably giving up your right to live there unless your husband specifically agrees to let you come back. If you're moving out and the children are staying with your husband, work out a visitation plan for the duration of your separation *before you leave*. (Work out a similar agreement if he's moving out.) And get it in writing.

Before you move out, also be sure to document everything that you can before you close the door behind you. Make photocopies of all financial records, and take pictures or a video of your property because once you leave, you may never have the opportunity to gather this information again. Also ask for records of improvements, repairs, and remodeling of your home. If you request them now, the court will make sure you get them. Even if you don't intend to use the information right away, ask for it now. If you wait until later in your divorce and then try to gather this paperwork, your husband may refuse to give it to you, and there may be nothing you can do at that point.

Financial Repercussions of Separating

Separation means more than just physically moving out. It means separating financial interests as well. You need to decide who will handle family expenses during the separation and who will pay for everything from insurance premiums to the orthodontist's bills. Again, the object is to maintain your previous standard of living during the separation. This will be important later on when you need to prove (either in negotiations or in court) exactly how much money you actually need to live on. If you live hand to mouth during the separation, you run the risk of living hand to mouth for many years after the divorce.

Credit Where It's Due

I talked earlier about the need to establish credit in your own name as soon as (or, better yet, before) you separate. Why is this so important? Because now that you're ready to begin your walk down the road to financial independence, the ability to establish credit in your own name lets you know that your goal is within reach.

First, take a good honest look at your credit record. Even if the overrun credit card limits on your joint accounts are your husband's fault, they are still debts that you share as a couple. And if the two of you have a poor credit rating, it will haunt you as well as him. Check the balances due on any outstanding bills and figure out the total sum that you owe. If you have credit cards that you don't share with your husband, include the balances on these, too.

When you start paying off your joint credit cards, use money from your joint account to do so even if you personally have more money than your husband does. Don't bend over backward to please your husband by paying off joint debts with your own money in the hope that he'll reward you either by staying married or by being scrupulously fair during future financial discussions. *Don't* fall into this way of thinking. It can become a bad habit—and a costly one.

As a general rule, don't cancel *any* credit cards until you've applied for credit in your own name. There are several options for establishing your own line of credit—an American Express Gold Card with a ten-thousand dollar limit is not the be-all and end-all route to credit card heaven.

The first order of business is to open a savings or checking account in your maiden name or your married name, whichever you plan to use after your divorce. If you and your husband haven't already separated, you can use the family assets and credit history (assuming it's good) to obtain credit in your own name. If you *have* already separated, you should change the billing on your utilities service to your own name—not your husband's—as soon as possible. Even something as simple as this can start you on the road to good credit.

Now you're ready to apply for your first credit card. Your best bet is a gasoline card, a department store card, or a Visa or MasterCard with a low credit limit. Ask willing friends or family members to co-sign on your account. This will make your friends or family members legally liable for your debt if you do not pay, so don't abuse the privilege or their trust.

You can also apply for a secured credit card, which is essentially the same as a Visa or MasterCard. The only difference is that a secured credit card is tied to your savings account, and your spending limit is generally linked to the balance in your account.

If you are denied credit when you first apply, keep reapplying. Don't give up. You are entitled to see a copy of your credit report as well as a written explanation of why you were denied. Finding the rough spots in your credit report can help you the next time around. If your husband's inability (or refusal) to pay his credit card debts is keeping you from obtaining credit, write a detailed letter to the credit bureau explaining that you are applying for a card in your own name based on your own credit history and that you are in the process of divorcing your husband and divesting yourself of legal liability for his past or present debts. (More about the legal and practical realities of dividing debt in Part III.)

Another way to improve your creditworthiness is by showing a record of employment. If you don't already have a job, try to get one. Obviously, it helps to have a job that you find personally, professionally, and financially rewarding. For the purpose of establishing credit, however, almost any respectable job will do. It doesn't have to be the job of the century, just some form of employment that indicates to a lender that you have a source of income and will be able to pay back the money extended to you on credit.

Once you have succeeded in getting one or more credit cards, be extra sure to pay your balance in full each month on each card. This is a great way to demonstrate your creditworthiness. And if you have been unable to obtain a Visa or MasterCard before, a squeaky clean credit history will certainly help when you reapply.

How to Handle Joint Accounts

Only after you have secured your own credit in your own name should you cancel your joint credit card accounts. Not before. Remember to close *all* joint accounts, even if you both own a particular credit card that only you use. Just because your husband has never used the Macy's charge before doesn't mean that he won't. It doesn't hurt to be extra cautious.

First, put the request in writing, asking not only that the accounts be closed but that you be notified of any outstanding charges. Then you can either choose to pay off the debts yourself or work out a system of payment with your husband. Once the balance has been paid in full, the accounts can be closed. Get your scissors out, cut your cards in half, and mail them back to whoever issued them. Let each creditor know in writing that you will not be responsible for any new charges. This is the only effective way to protect yourself against future debts that you don't know about and don't want to know about.

Dealing with joint accounts also involves the disposition of bank and brokerage accounts and deciding how these will be handled during the Decision stage. It simplifies matters if you and your husband maintain separate bank accounts and separate brokerage accounts. But if your accounts remain in joint ownership, you should make absolutely sure that your husband gets your signed consent before he does anything that could directly affect you. Write a letter posthaste to your banker, broker, and to all others with whom you or your husband have a financial relationship, letting them know that you are separated. This is critically important because either party on a joint account is legally authorized to give instructions on that account unless the banker or broker is informed otherwise in writing. (More about handling bank and brokerage accounts below.)

Equity Credit Lines

Equity credit lines aren't tied to your bank account like most credit cards. Instead, they give you check writing privileges based on the value of your house. If you have an equity line of credit, write to the bank immediately and freeze the account. That way you can protect yourself against your husband's writing checks and depleting the equity in your home without your knowledge. This doesn't mean you're taking the money out and leaving your husband up a creek; it's simply preventing him from doing this to you. You should not risk losing your home just because you overlooked this line of credit.

Brokerage Accounts

If you and your husband have joint brokerage accounts, you should notify the brokerage firm in writing immediately that you and your husband have separated. Specify that the broker should not buy, sell, or send checks out unless instructions come from both signatures on the account. The branch manager of the brokerage firm will then inform your husband in writing that these instructions have been received and are on record. From that time on, the brokerage firm will take instructions only from both parties on the account, not from you alone or from your husband alone.

This is especially important if you have a margin account, which allows you to borrow money from the brokerage firm to make additional investments. By investing with borrowed money that's not really yours, you're not only liable for repaying the debt but for interest on the debt as well. This is especially problematic if the investments don't pan out and you end up selling at a loss. You can see how important it is to prevent the possibility of your husband's turning your brokerage account into a debt nightmare. Write to your broker immediately.

You don't want to end up in the same boat as my client Gloria whose husband of thirty-seven years decided to start trading commodities at another brokerage firm soon after their separation. He managed to lose more than $20,000 before Gloria even realized what was going on.

Joint Bank Accounts

You have several options when it comes to joint bank accounts. Depending on your temporary agreement during the divorce proceedings, you may decide to leave money in joint accounts. For example, if you are staying in your house but have plans to sell it at a later date and split the proceeds, you'll need to maintain the value of this asset by continuing to mow the lawn, get the trees trimmed, fix the broken shutters, paint the interior, and so forth. As I mentioned earlier, in order to make sure that you both get the best possible price when you do sell, the house has to be maintained in good condition. Keeping a joint account can allow you to access funds to maintain the house without eating up the financial resources you need to live on.

Then again, there are other ways to divide financial responsibilities while you're separated. For example, if the numbers pencil out, you can pay for the upkeep on the house and your husband pay for your children's school tuition. In this event, a joint account is not always necessary. Sometimes it feels better psychologically to begin making a clean break, and closing joint accounts can give you your first taste of liberation from a bad marriage. Think about what works for you and what's in your best financial and emotional interest.

If you *do* decide to keep a joint account open, you're entitled to half of whatever's in it. If you feel vulnerable—you may be worried that your husband won't pay the temporary alimony he promised—or if you need cash right away to put down first and last months' rent on an apartment, you may decide to withdraw your share of the money immediately. Many women opt not to do this, however, because they worry about seeming too greedy or too adversarial. If they can get by without taking out their half of the joint funds, they choose to keep things on more amicable terms now in the hope of keeping the peace later. For my money, that's wishful thinking.

If you do decide not to move your half of the money out of

the account, you should certainly protect yourself against the possibility of finding it empty three months down the road. You don't want to see your husband sporting a new Rolex while you're left without grocery money. It's not unheard of. Guard against this happening by instructing your bank to freeze the account. This means both your signatures will be needed to take money out of the account, so you'll be protected against your husband's withdrawing money while you're not looking.

Assessing Your State of Mind: Where Am I Coming From?

All of the to-do lists notwithstanding, what is most important at this stage is *you*. More than once during the Decision phase (which can feel pretty much like entering the Twilight Zone), you'll probably want to turn the phone off, curl up under a warm blanket, and sleep for about ten years—until all of this is ancient history. Maybe then an oh-so handsome Mr. Wonderful will swing by in a white convertible, and the two of you will ride off into the sunset and everything will be A-OK. Dreaming can be therapeutic and a lot more fun than living in reality, but at some point you'll have to deal with the wake-up call of seemingly endless—but all too real—tasks that mark the passage from "we" to "me." And some of them will be major eye-openers.

In preparing both emotionally and financially for divorce, an important first step is to reacquaint you with yourself. This doesn't mean three-way mirrors and long questionnaires. It means knowing and understanding where you're coming from so you'll know where you need and want to go.

Many women don't take an active role in family finances, either through lack of interest or lack of opportunity. No wonder they don't know whom to turn to now for financial and legal advice or just about anything else. You may not know where financial documents are located or even what they look like, and, like most women beginning the "business" of divorce, you probably don't want to deal with any of this. You wish it would all just go away.

It's important to be honest with yourself—starting today. Know where you're most vulnerable and which issues are likely to be hardest to cope with. Coming to terms with your own reality will help you deal with your divorce more successfully and with much greater strength. I promise you'll get through this. You *will* live to tell about it.

Where Am I Going?

From a financial perspective, the best way to figure out where you're going is to get to know your "money self." And the best way to get to know your money self is to ask yourself: How confident am I about handling money? Even if you didn't prepare the family tax return or run a million-dollar business, you probably know a lot more about money management than you think you do. Chances are, you balanced the family budget, made most of the major household purchases, and were responsible for buying groceries and clothing for the entire family. No small feat these days.

Did you pay the bills and make deposits to the checking and savings accounts? Did you ever borrow money or co-sign on a loan? Did you use credit cards or any other kind of revolving account? You probably dealt with money a lot more often than you realize or give yourself credit for. Preparing to handle the rest is just expanding on what you already do know. The same dollar sense and judgment apply.

Think about who earned the money in your marriage, who managed it, and who controlled it. If you worked outside the home, think about what you did with your paycheck. Did you deposit it into a joint account and use it to pay bills? Or was it kept separately as "fun money"? My client Sandi's income was earmarked for vacations and other "extras." While it was nice that her husband earned enough for both of them to live on and provide for their two daughters, I couldn't help thinking that the implication was that *her income didn't count.* It wasn't treated as "serious money" but instead was used strictly for the fun stuff. By extension, her job as a preschool teacher wasn't taken too seriously, either. It ultimately became a point of pride for her husband to boast that *he* supported the family but approved of Sandi's job because "it keeps her busy and lets her earn a little pin money."

As you continue to get acquainted with your money self, think about whether you kept any assets or financial instruments—credit cards, bank accounts, and so forth—in your name alone. How financially dependent or independent were you during your marriage? Your confidence or lack of confidence about handling money is likely to be directly proportionate to how much financial jurisdiction you had during your marriage.

Next, while you're still in the honesty chair, think about how you're handling things emotionally. How do you feel about taking responsibility for your own financial future and perhaps your children's as well? Scared, nauseated, and wanting to run away and hide are all perfectly reasonable answers, but that will change as you grow more confident about handling your money, yourself, and your life after divorce. Don't worry about how strong and emotionally together you think you're *supposed* to be right now. Just let yourself feel what you feel without criticizing or judging.

Getting Help When You Need Help: Counseling

If you're having trouble dealing with some of these feelings or with life altogether, consider going for professional counseling. Here is the place where you can discuss your feelings openly and without reservation. Don't hold back. Vent your hostility, blame your husband for messing everything up, fantasize about revenge. Anything and everything you feel is okay to talk about. Your therapist's office can be your safe harbor in a roiling sea of legal documents and lawyerspeak—and an excellent source of free Kleenex! At a time when you have to weigh and measure every thought and feeling and decide whether it belongs in your lawyer's office or is for primal screaming in the shower, your therapist can help you find a truly appropriate place for what you're feeling. And later on, counseling will help you keep your anger out of your settlement negotiations and in the therapist's office where it can be healing rather than destructive.

You also might consider a support group for divorced and divorcing women. This is not about "misery loves company." It's about sharing your feelings and experiences with other women who can completely identify with you. You don't have to explain anything to them—they understand. Support groups are so named because they provide tremendous support at a time when it's critically important and inordinately valuable.

But don't make the mistake of thinking that you'll be relegated to a social life spent exclusively with other divorced and divorcing women. The last thing you need is to sit around and talk about your divorce all day, every day. While other divorced women can help because they've been through what you're going through, they don't have to constitute your only social life. A divorce support group is fine as long as it's for support—not the basis of your life.

It's also important to let your friends be there for you. Don't throw out married friends along with your marriage. Some of them may feel torn between you and your husband, but don't assume that they can't be good friends to you even if they're still friends with him.

And don't assume that your married friends will shudder at the thought of spending time with you socially now that you're no longer one-half of a couple. While there are always exceptions, most people will view you as their friend first, a divorced or divorcing woman second. Besides, if they like spending time with other couples, maybe they can fix you up with someone they know if you're interested! There's plenty of time for all that, so if not now, maybe later.

Attack of the Not-So-Great Ideas

The most important thing you can do for yourself during the Decision stage and throughout your divorce is to be honest about where you are and where you think you're going. Resist the temptation to grasp the quick fix that may seem like a light-bulb over your head at the moment but won't shine so brightly later on. And be wary of the following not-so-great ideas:

Not-So-Great Idea Number 1: Don't call a lawyer, don't do anything! Just stay tuned because you're sure to be rescued as soon as the village maidens finish braiding the flower buds onto that beautiful white horse's mane. And that stallion will be galloping over any minute, complete with a nice, good-looking, sensitive guy riding high in the saddle who is just like your husband in all the good ways and totally opposite in all the bad ways. He'll help you breeze through the divorce by making all the hard decisions for you, and you'll never have to deal with any of this again.

Why It Won't Work: Whoa there! What if Prince Charming turns out to be Prince Charmless? Either way, by falling head-long into a new relationship, you're robbing yourself of the chance to get to know who you really are—to reach a state of true independence where you can take on a new relationship from a place of strength rather than from a place of vulnerability.

Not-So-Great Idea Number 2: You still believe that men should support their wives—even their ex-wives—and you shouldn't ask, and shouldn't have to worry about, the family finances even post-divorce.

Why It Won't Work: If you do still believe this, think long and hard about how well this attitude has served you in the past and why you think things will be any different in the future.

Not-So-Great Idea Number 3: Money isn't feminine. If you become too financially savvy, it will put men off, make them feel threatened, and seriously injure your chances for a new relationship. And anyway, it's too hard for a woman in a "man's world" to handle her own finances without getting talked down to or, worse, ripped off.

Why It Won't Work: Money is an equal opportunity employer. It's genderless. Women today are handling everything from making financial decisions for their families to managing complex investment portfolios. And women are working outside the home in record numbers. For years the world of money *was* a man's world, but it isn't anymore. Nor is it unfeminine. If old thinking still persists in some circles, it's up to us to change it, not embrace it.

Not-So-Great Idea Number 4: It's not worth fighting about money. You'd rather learn to live on less than go to war with your husband. And you certainly don't want one of those long-drawn-out divorces with everyone incessantly arguing about who gets what. If you've never worked outside the home and he's always earned the money, maybe he *should* get more. You're not sure what you're entitled to anyway, and it's just too irritating haggling over every dime.

Why It Won't Work: You've contributed to your marriage, too. Perhaps in ways less readily quantifiable than the dollars your husband has earned, but your contribution counts. Women still earn lower wages than men (at last count, $.76 to the dollar for the same job), so even if you both worked outside the home, odds are that your income was lower than his. Get over the idea that you're asking for something that isn't yours. It's just not true. You're asking for what you're entitled to, what you deserve. And don't underestimate how much money you'll need to live on post-divorce. Before you jump the gun and start making financial concessions left and right, run the numbers. Don't make promises that your checkbook can't keep.

Not-So-Great Idea Number 5: Going to work won't pay off, because you'll either just owe a lot of money in taxes or will hate your job. You'd rather let someone else worry about bringing home the bacon. You'll stick to cooking it.

Why It Won't Work: In the 1990s, the question of whether to work or not to work has almost become a moot point. Most households need two incomes just to survive in today's economy. So even if you do remarry, you may not be able to avoid the workplace forever. Besides, why miss the chance to find out what you can accomplish as your own person? Even if you choose not to work but are forced to by economic necessity, view it as an opportunity. Make it a positive rather than a negative, and go for it.

Now that you've promised yourself to avoid the quick fixes and the not-so-great-ideas, you're ready to move forward. The Planning Period that comes next will take some clear thinking and your firm resolve to get what you want and what you deserve. Stay calm, stay tuned. You can do this!

PART II

• • •

The Planning Period

Together but Moving Apart

●●●

The Planning Period begins when one or both of you has absolutely, finally decided to call it quits. It's no longer "Maybe we'll get divorced." It's "We're getting divorced." For certain. For positive. For real.

The decision to end the marriage has now been made, but the emotional, legal, and financial wrangling has only just begun. It's like the quiet before the storm. And you feel as though the storm you're waiting for is a torrential downpour fit for Noah's ark—which has just set sail without you. That's okay. Remember the rainbow. You're going to get through this.

The hard part is recognizing that you and your husband have different interests and different agendas now. You're not on the same team anymore, and that can feel pretty strange and can sometimes get downright ugly. Especially when the financial stakes are high, you'll find emotional issues manifesting themselves in knock-down, drag-out arguments over "That's mine and you can't have it!" Or the flip side, you'll feel as if you're the only one who's upset about the marriage breaking up while your cool-as-a-cucumber husband is clear-headed enough to start divvying up the money. Does that mean he's feeling no emotional pain whatsoever? Maybe, but not likely. While you may be more prone to tears and anger, his feelings may surface big time in competitiveness and control over financial issues.

The Planning Period is a time when you're apt to feel overwhelmed at every turn. You've done the preliminary footwork, but the reality of the whole divorce process looms before you. The best way to get through it is one step at a time. Divorce is a difficult journey, but for many women it's the road to a much better place.

Getting through the Planning Period means living with the realization that your divorce *is* going forward. It's going to happen. It's a soon-to-be-done deal. You may feel sadness and anger because your marriage couldn't be salvaged. Sometimes solace comes in the form of Ben & Jerry's Triple Brownie Overload. Sometimes it comes by way of staying in bed for three days straight, watching "Mary Tyler Moore" reruns on Nickelodeon. ("How will you make it on your own?") But eventually you'll get out of bed, rinse off your ice cream spoon, and begin to get on with your life. It's during this breathing period, after you've agreed to *start* the divorce but before the major financial wrangling begins, that you can collect yourself and prepare for the months ahead.

For some women this is a time of pain and loneliness; for others it's a time of exhilaration, a time for experiencing freedom for the first time in a long time. Some women take to shopping with abandon or going on self-improvement sprees. You may feel an overwhelming need to redefine your self-image, and some new clothes and a new look may be a welcome change and a terrific ego boost. Just be careful not to boost your ego by burying yourself in debt.

The best way to prepare yourself for the rest of your divorce is by getting emotionally prepared during the Planning Period. Try to anticipate the feelings before they sneak up on you. It's like PMS—you know it's coming and you know there's a perfectly valid explanation for every confusing or contradictory emotion that you're feeling, but that doesn't mean you can stop it from happening. It just means you can sometimes step back and understand that it's okay, it's part of the process and it will pass.

When Smoke Gets in Your Eyes

Right now everything has a sentimental tint to it. The collection of heart-shaped Limoges boxes that you bought on your honeymoon and even the Andy Warhol print that you don't really like become till-death-do-us-part emotional attachments. How will you divide it all up? And if your husband insists on having it, how will you ever live without the grandfather clock that consistently chimes the hour exactly four minutes late? Now is the time to stop and think about your possessions and what they really mean to you. Do you truly feel like you can't live without them, or can you comfortably let go of some of them? There may be some things you're particularly attached to, things you feel you absolutely must have. If so, make a special effort to act nonchalant about them for the time being. You don't want your husband to use this attachment against you, to convince you to give up your share of the bond portfolio because he knows how much you want your grandmother's china. You can work out the details later, but for now, keep a poker face when items of particular interest are being discussed.

And beware of making premature concessions because you're feeling guilty, especially if you're not at fault. Don't let guilt immobilize you—or mobilize you into the wrong kind of action. As hard as it may be, you need to internalize the fact that *you* didn't ruin your marriage. There may be many reasons why it didn't work, but you alone were not the root cause of all the problems. Don't ever feel that you need to pay somehow for the fact that the marriage didn't work. Divorce is not about giving up on your future because you're down in the dumps right now. It's about guaranteeing that your future will be a whole lot better than your present—or your past.

Part of securing your future means preventing your husband from single-handedly controlling the divorce process. That's why you have your "A team." Remember, your "A team" is working for you and on your behalf, but ultimately the buck stops with you. You need to stay in control of each money issue. And if your husband begins using emotional manipulation to persuade you to do something that's not in your best interest, don't give in. You have to fight for what you want. Fight fairly if he's fighting fairly, but don't be shocked if his tactics don't exactly conform to Marquess of Queensberry rules.

Please remember that it doesn't make sense to settle for less than you deserve just to end the divorce more quickly. True, you've decided to go forward with your new life, and it's tempting to want that life to begin as soon as possible. But here's where you'll have to be patient and trust that it will pay off later. Now is the time to set up your future "life plan." Later is the time to reap the rewards. Don't shortchange your future by making hasty decisions today. You don't want to end up two years from now hitting yourself over the head and saying, "What was I thinking?"

"I couldn't deal with the tension," admits Anne, thirty-two, reflecting on her divorce of three years ago. "I know for a fact that I didn't get what I deserved. I hired the best divorce lawyer in town and didn't let him do his job. He told me his hands were tied because I cared more about not upsetting my husband than I did about getting what was rightfully mine." Anne says this today with great regret, even though time has allowed the rawest of her emotional wounds to heal, and she can honestly say that she has been much happier since her divorce than she ever was during her marriage. Still, three years after the fact, she wishes she had done things differently.

"Everything started getting ugly, and I couldn't handle it," recalls Anne. "Too many tears, too much aggravation, too much pain. After a while, I couldn't stand it anymore, so I gave in to whatever my husband wanted. My lawyer said I just rolled over and played dead. When I think back on it, he was probably right."

Why did Anne "roll over" when it clearly wasn't in her own best interest to do so? "Jim and I were high school sweethearts," she explains. "And when someone you've loved for over twenty years accuses you of trying to take him for everything he's worth, it's hard *not* to roll over. I didn't want him to think I was out to bleed him dry," she says.

The Cruella de Ville scenario strikes again. Sound familiar?

Moving Forward

The Planning Period is about letting go of your past. And, most important, it's about planning for the future. Ultimately, it's about your new life, a life in which each decision you make is about increasing your happiness, your independence, your self-worth, and your net worth.

My Two C's and Two D's: A Money Philosophy That Will Guide You Through Divorce and Through Life

In considering the money philosophy I use to advise women about managing their finances, I realized that the same philosophy could also help women make moneysmart decisions during the divorce process. We all have very basic needs for emotional well-being and financial security: common sense in making decisions, comfort with what we've decided, diversification in all facets of our lives, and discipline to pursue our goals and keep ourselves on the right track.

Since these familiar basics work so well for successful living, not only can they be applied to money management, but they can also act as your reality check when you're going through the divorce process.

I've created four categories, which I call the Two C's and Two D's: common sense, comfort level, diversification, and discipline. Think of the Two C's and Two D's when you come up against any major divorce decision or dilemma. This philosophy will help keep you emotionally grounded while providing you with a sound basis for making moneysmart decisions.

The First C: Common Sense

Your first guideline for making divorce decisions is nothing more than relying on your common sense. It means stopping every once in a while and asking yourself, "Does this make sense?"

As you go through the divorce process, it seems as though everyone around you has an opinion about just about everything. Your lawyer recommends that you do one thing. Your best friend recommends the exact opposite. And your daughter's fifth grade homeroom teacher can't wait to tell you all about the mistakes she made during her own divorce. If you let yourself be confused by the gazillion opinions buzzing around you, you may end up making decisions that make sense to everyone else but you. Remember, it's everyone's God-given right to try to make you crazy. It's your God-given right to decline to be made crazy.

Just because your cousin Penny's husband hid assets from her doesn't mean that your husband is hiding money from you, so take what she says with a grain of salt. If you have no concerns about numbers that don't add up or mysterious expenses that never cropped up before, you may be safe in assuming that there aren't any hidden assets to worry about—especially if you dealt with the money matters and were always in the financial loop during your marriage. So if your lawyer recommends hiring an expensive forensic accountant to go out and look for underhanded dealings, remember to apply the first C: Does it really make sense?

Similarly, when you begin dividing assets, you'll hear opinions from here to eternity about what you should keep. Maybe your attorney thinks stocks are a prime asset to keep. But your attorney isn't you. Do stocks make you comfortable? Or does losing money in the stock market make you want to lose your lunch? Are there other assets you'd much rather have? No matter what your attorney, your father, or your butcher's wife says, your settlement strategy needs to make sense to you. Just because your coworker, Joanie, negotiated long and hard to keep her valuable and much-cherished sterling silver doesn't mean that you should do the same. If you don't enjoy entertaining and prefer stock certificates to a matched set of cutlery any day of the week, go for the stock and forget the flatwear. The assets you keep are yours to sell, manage, or give away. In some cases, they'll be yours to have and to hold from this day forward, so make sure to use your common sense when it comes to figuring out what you want.

The Second C: Comfort Zone

Your second guideline for successfully surviving your divorce comes from the mouth of my grandmother who always said, "If it doesn't feel good, don't do it." This is a terrific philosophy for life and certainly an excellent philosophy for this time of your life.

In fact, feeling comfortable with your divorce decisions is so important that even if it means going against the advice of your family, friends, or financial advisers, you should always stay within your comfort zone. Listen to—and trust—your own instincts.

Maybe your mother thinks you should hold out for a lump sum settlement, but your husband won't budge from insisting on monthly alimony payments instead. Should you listen to your mom even if it means going to court to get the lump sum settlement? Maybe, maybe not. If you fight hard for this, are you less likely to get the lifetime country club membership that is so important to you? Or maybe you'd rather have trusts set up ensuring that your husband will pay for your children's college education and postgraduate studies than argue about the form in which your settlement is to be paid.

Remember, if it doesn't feel right, don't be so quick to follow someone else's advice. Ultimately, it's your settlement, and it has to feel good to you. You are the one who has to live with the decisions that you make.

I see a major difference between men and women and the money decisions they make based on their respective comfort levels. The same is certainly true during divorce. Here is where men and women definitely part company. It has been my experience that men tend to think with their wallets, women with their hearts.

It all comes back to the issue of money and power. Far too often, for men, divorce is about who controls whom—and who controls the bucks. Sometimes it becomes a contest. If he can get you to roll over during the negotiation process, he'll feel like he's won. For some men it's "hero or zero" time.

For most women, divorce isn't about power and winning. It's about ending a marriage and losing a relationship—in many cases, a lifelong relationship. So even though it's important to hold your ground, remember to play by *your* rules, not his. And if it doesn't feel good, don't do it.

The First D: Diversification

Diversification is Wall Street-ese for "don't put all your eggs in one basket." When you diversify, you're taking your comfort level one step further—especially during the negotiation period. The idea is that even if you're comfortable keeping a specific asset (your house, for example), you should not ignore the potential value of the other assets that you and your husband own (like your tax-free bond portfolio).

Also, if you are to receive your entire settlement in the form of alimony—which your husband could "forget" to pay— you're at risk. What if it takes months for the court to force him to pay, but your mortgage payment was due last week? Make sure to have a backup plan just in case. Use a Qualified Domestic Relations Order (QDRO) to ensure that you'll get paid out of his pension plan assets if he's delinquent on alimony payments. (The QDRO is explained in detail on page 127.)

And if your share of the settlement includes part or all of an investment portfolio, diversification is critical here. Depending on your specific financial needs, you may ultimately want to own bonds that can provide you with monthly income, or stocks that can offer you growth opportunities. Ideally, of course, you should own both. (We'll talk more about stocks, bonds, and diversification in Part IV.)

The Second D: Discipline

Discipline is the single most important component of my Two C's and Two D's philosophy, especially when you're deluged with well-meaning advice and opinions from everyone and her sister about how you should handle your divorce. Once you've made decisions that feel right, make sense, and provide you with a diversified group of assets, don't listen to anyone who insists on telling you that you've completely messed up. If people have an overdeveloped need to run your life, that's their problem. Don't make it yours.

Knowing exactly what you want requires discipline. And it means taking the time to think things through and formulate a plan. Think about making ends meet today and think about retirement down the road. Think about yourself and think

about your children. There *is* a good, common-sense plan out
there for you.

Your Five- and Ten-Year Life Plan: How to Get Started

Today *is* the first day of the rest of your life. Your five-year and
ten-year life plan begins today. And the sooner you take control of your divorce, the sooner you can get on with your life
plan.

Start now by keeping on top of each stage of your divorce
and knowing what action to take. During the Planning Period
it's important to maintain your previous standard of living to
the best of your ability just as it was during the Decision stage
and just as it will be throughout your separation and divorce
proceedings. This is critically important for your children's
morale as well as your own. Don't make the mistake of casting
your husband in the role of Daddy Warbucks while you play
the cheapo mom who's always saying, "No, we don't have
enough money."

If you haven't already done so, now is the time to start negotiating for temporary alimony and child support so you can
get through this difficult period. Best case is to have these
arrangements in place before one of you moves out, but it's
certainly a must now. This is especially important if you don't
work outside the home. Why should you feel like a bag lady
begging for handouts? Get what you're entitled to and don't
apologize for asking.

If you plan to enter or reenter the job market or to make
any other career move, your life plan may include taking
classes or visiting a career counselor if you didn't already do
so during the Decision stage. If you can afford it, take your
time before making any decisions that affect your long-term
financial security. If you can't, do what you have to do.

Many of your life decisions will revolve around money,
even the most joyful and long-awaited life events. Doesn't it

seem as though everything touches on money issues sooner or later? Your children graduating from high school and going on to college and your parents' fiftieth wedding anniversary both have financial repercussions for you. Who will pay for your son's college education, much less your daughter's law school tuition? And who will take care of your seventy-five-year-old parents when their retirement savings run out?

Making a Plan and Checking It Twice

This may be as good a time as any to start thinking about what lies ahead financially, not just for your family but for you. If you have been planning to go back to school, you'll need to find the time and money to do so. If you'll be planning a bar mitzvah for your son in two years, keep that expense in mind. If you have a balloon payment on your house coming due within the next five years, think about how you'll pay for it. Keeping track of life events that you know about in advance will certainly help you when you negotiate your divorce settlement. It's impossible to plan ahead for the surprises that are always part of life, but at least you can plan for the sure things.

Begin by making a list. Include any financial commitments you know you'll have within the next five years and in the next ten. Write down what each commitment is, when you think it will arise, and how much you need to budget to meet it. Put them in order of priority, whether in a timeline (which comes first) or a money line (which costs most).

Next, think about where the money has come from to meet similar expenses in the past. Have you and your husband borrowed to cover major life expenses? Has it come from your earnings? His paycheck?

Then think about how much money it's costing you to live right now. Where is that money coming from? Is your husband footing all the bills? If so, good for you. You're among the lucky few. Some women do manage to rely solely on temporary alimony during divorce proceedings, saving anything they can from their own paychecks to use later. But that's wishful thinking for most women for whom temporary alimony is barely enough to meet living expenses. Some women are even forced to sell assets to pay for the basics of life. Others borrow up to the limit on their credit cards and get into debt way over their heads.

Don't get into this kind of financial pickle. Identifying your spending patterns and thinking about how you pay for things now will help you make a realistic, common-sense plan for a future that works. Documenting what you spend and where the money is coming from (maybe you're dipping into savings each month—a temporary solution at best) will also help when you negotiate your final settlement. You are more likely to get what you need to live on if you're clear on the amount.

Just the Facts, Ma'am

It's time to get down to the nitty-gritty. You need to figure out the total amount of income you rely on now. Some of it may come from your paycheck and some from your husband's. If either of you typically receives a year-end bonus, list that in a separate category from regular salary. And don't forget to include any supplementary income earned by moonlighting or through a combination of small jobs, from tutoring math to giving tennis lessons. Maybe you count on interest income on bonds or dividends on stocks that you own. Don't leave anything out. Be sure to write down all sources of income and the amount generated.

Next, calculate your expenses. The easiest way to do this is by sitting down with your checkbook entries and receipts from the last six months, including credit card statements. Add up everything that you spent money on for the last six months and divide it by six to get your monthly average.

Based on this figure, you can determine your yearly expenses—just multiply by twelve. To make this number as accurate as possible, remember to include expenses like car insurance that you may pay semi-annually or school tuition that you probably pay annually. If you have kids, it's a good idea to divide your expenses into general family living expenses and expenses specifically relating to your children. Once you have some actual numbers to look at, you can approach the settlement process with information and intelligence. And when you negotiate for temporary support, you'll have facts and figures to help you get what you need to live on during this interim period before you draft your final settlement.

Keeping It All Together—Temporary Support

All agreements for temporary alimony and child support should be in writing in a formal legal document signed by the court.

During your separation you'll need money to live on. And, as I've said earlier, the more able you are to maintain your previous standard of living, the better. Begin by requesting temporary alimony. You will have to pay taxes on it, and it will definitely be factored in when dividing your assets later on, but it can also make the difference between paying your bills on time and getting yourself into financial hot water.

If you and your husband can agree on how much temporary support you'll need, you're in good shape. If your husband won't willingly pay you temporary alimony, you'll need to go to court immediately. Your attorney can help you file for temporary alimony and child support, and the court will decide how much your husband needs to pay.

This is not to say that it's the husband who does the paying in all cases. Sometimes the shoe is on the other foot and it's the wife who foots the bill for alimony and, in rare instances, even child support if the husband has been awarded temporary custody. (You may recall the widespread publicity in 1992 when Joan Lunden was ordered to pay her estranged husband $18,000 plus in monthly maintenance.) Still, most women today are on the receiving rather than on the paying end of the equation, although many struggle to make ends meet even with alimony and child support, which is all too often inadequate.

Now you'll see why it's so essential to have a good estimate of your monthly expenses, including the legal fees that you're now paying. You should understand that although temporary support is used as a basis for considering the amount of permanent support, the amount you are awarded now may well be higher than the amount you receive in your final settlement. You should also be aware of the fact that getting a court order doesn't guarantee that you'll actually receive the money. If your husband refuses to pay, you'll have to resort to other methods to meet your financial needs during the divorce proceedings.

If you need to borrow money or sell some of your personal property to pay for your basic living expenses, keep track of every penny that you spend. You can negotiate to recover these expenses later on when you divide your joint assets during the settlement negotiation.

It is also legally possible to sell joint assets if you need to raise cash immediately. You'll need your husband's signature, as he would need yours to do the same. Assuming he agrees to let you sell, you can go ahead and do so. Remember, though, that in the final settlement, he will be entitled to cash or other assets of equal value to those you've already sold. If there aren't assets of equal value, you may have to hold off on selling anything until your settlement agreement is completed. For example, the family home is the most valuable asset of most couples. If you decide to sell your house and live on the proceeds during your divorce proceedings, it's highly unlikely that there will be a comparable asset that can be designated as your husband's. The moral of the story is that if you need to raise cash, the easiest way to do so is by selling an asset that can easily be divided fifty-fifty. It's a simple matter to sell one hundred shares of XYZ stock if you and your husband together own a total of two hundred shares.

Supporting Your Children

To make sure you get the amount of temporary support you need for your children and don't get shortchanged, it's important to have an accurate estimate of what you actually spend on them. Aside from the obvious food and clothing expenses, don't forget to include team jerseys and sports equipment, piano lessons, school supplies, flu shots, orthodontia, and weekly allowances. If you and your husband typically took your kids to the movies once a week or sent them to sleep-away camp every summer, they are entitled to maintain that lifestyle after you separate. Your kids shouldn't have to settle for less—and neither should you.

Each state has individual guidelines to help calculate how much financial support you will need for the number of children you have. The court will examine your request for child support to make sure it is consistent with your children's best interest.

That's all well and good, but the bad news is that just because the court awards you child support doesn't mean you'll automatically get it from your husband. "Deadbeat dads" who fail to pay or are consistently behind on child support payments are becoming all too common.

Don't think you're going to improve the situation by bad-mouthing your husband in front of your kids or denying him visitation rights if you have custody. You're more likely to just alienate your children or force them into a position of having to defend Dad. This is a no-win situation for you. For your kids' sake, save your battles for the courtroom or the lawyers' offices. This is where the major negotiating begins. So don't waste time duking it out with him on your front doorstep in full view of your children. Frankly, it's not worth the effort.

The Road to Discovery

Simply stated, discovery is the process of gathering documents and information about what you and your husband own. In plain English, it's the meat and potatoes of getting divorced. The process of legal discovery in and of itself does not have to be lengthy or difficult. The fact that it often gets that way has more to do with super-heated emotions than confusion over what assets you and your husband own. Theoretically, if the two of you can agree on what you own, what your assets are worth, which of your property is separate and which is marital, and what each of you will get in your divorce settlement, the discovery phase is merely a time to get all this down in writing.

If only it were so easy.

Unfortunately, as emotions flare, so do arguments over who should keep which assets and what these things are really worth. If your husband feels put upon or combative after long go-rounds with the lawyers, he may take it out on you by being obstinate and arbitrarily difficult. No, you can't have the dining room chairs even though you know he's always hated them and has absolutely no use for them. They're worth a lot more than you think they are, he'll say, and he's always loved them. Yeah, right—on what planet? Frustration upon frustration. And the longer discovery takes, the more you may feel like you're going three steps backward for every one step forward. And getting nowhere fast.

What Exactly Is Discovery?

There are actually several aspects to the discovery phase of your divorce. Although the term itself sounds like some fantastic archeological dig or a space shuttle to the stars, remember that discovery is really just a legalese term for the time used to discover what you own, what you owe, and what you ultimately want from your divorce settlement. It's a time for asking questions, getting the answers, gathering documents (if you haven't already done so), and taking oral statements (called depositions). The best thing you can do for yourself at this stage is to be completely open and honest with your lawyer. Don't be afraid of saying the wrong thing, and don't hold back information for fear your lawyer will think badly of you. Most important: If you think there is something your husband could use against you, it's critical to get it out in the open with your attorney now rather than risk an ambush by your husband's attorney later on.

During discovery, your lawyer will need to gather and have access to any and all financial documents, statements, and lists of property. If you've done some of this footwork during the Decision stage, you'll be able to provide a lot of this information yourself. What you don't already know, your lawyer and accountant will discover for you and with you. Both you and your husband will be required to complete a case information statement that identifies any income and assets that you each have.

During discovery, you and your husband will be asked to provide many documents that you may already be familiar with: bank statements, paycheck stubs, proof of ownership of assets, a statement of debts, and complete tax returns. Along with this information, your lawyer (or his) may want actual physical proof that certain assets exist. You may have to prove that the antique hutch in the dining room is filled with Waterford crystal. So plan on taking photos or providing a videotape as evidence. Beyond this, your lawyer can issue a request for inspection to gain physical access to possessions that either you or your husband holds. If you've kept the Limoges heart-shaped boxes, your husband's lawyer can send a request for inspection so their existence and value can be determined.

If you and your husband can agree on the value of the assets that you own, this figure will be recorded during discovery. If you cannot agree, the attorneys will request formal appraisals of all property, businesses, and other assets that you both own.

Depositions, Interrogatories, and Subpoenas

Part of the discovery process includes taking depositions, which involves answering questions under oath. If you suspect that your husband has hidden assets, this is an excellent time to ask about them. Your lawyer may also use interrogatories, which are written questions that must be answered in writing under oath. Interrogatories are often used, at least preliminarily, for assembling lists of bank accounts, brokerage accounts, and other financial assets.

Finally comes the subpoena. This legal procedure is used to call in any witness who can furnish information involving you or your husband. The classic example, so overdone in B movies and television dramas, is subpoenaing the blonde bombshell, Kim Basinger look-alike girlfriend. Of course, sometimes life does imitate art. If you *do* suspect your husband of having an affair, you will want to subpoena the woman with whom you think he's involved. If you suspect he has created fictitious "employees" to whom he pays phantom salaries every month, your lawyer will subpoena someone who works at your husband's office to provide a statement under oath. Even if there is no suspicion of underhandedness, subpoenas can be used to obtain documents from banks, credit card companies, or insurance companies as well as earnings reports from brokerage firms.

Be sure to review any statements made by your husband concerning the value that he places on certain assets and the amount of income generated from his job or business. If you think he has underestimated what he earns, your attorney can do some extensive questioning and fact-finding to ferret out hidden income.

The essential purpose of discovery is to prepare you for the next step in the divorce process, and the next one after that. Ultimately, all of this preparation will culminate in a property settlement agreement, which is a signed statement of consent outlining how your joint property will be divided in your divorce settlement. But let's not put the cart before the horse. Before you start dividing joint property, you need to know what constitutes joint property in your state.

In What State Are Your Finances? What You Get Depends on Where You Live

All things being equal, it shouldn't make a hill-of-beans difference to your divorce whether you live in New York, New Mexico, California, or Connecticut. But it does, and it's too late to move now. For future reference, though, try to avoid relocating to Mississippi. And if you live there now, think about moving after the divorce.

Why? Because in the state of Mississippi the laws governing joint property employ the principles of *common law*. Under this law, property is divided strictly according to who owns it. This means that if your husband holds legal title to both cars in his name only, they're both legally his. And if the house is in his name only, he doesn't have to divide it with you when you file for divorce. I know that these are not glad tidings for those of you who live in Mississippi, but they are the sad-but-true facts.

Community Property

There are nine states—Arizona, California, Idaho, Louisiana, Nevada, New Mexico, Texas, Washington, and Wisconsin—where marital assets are governed by community property laws.

If you live in one of these states, any property that you and your husband acquired while you were married is considered community (joint) property. All community property is divided equally when you get divorced except when the court decides that this would be inherently unfair. For example, a person who is considered "at fault" in the divorce might be awarded less than 50 percent of the joint assets.

Community property states recognize as "separate property" all property that you alone are entitled to keep after your divorce. To put it in its simplest terms, anything that you owned before you got married is yours to keep afterward. If it came with you, it leaves with you. The same is true for anything that you bought during your marriage using money that you had before you got married, or using money acquired by selling pre-marriage property. This is also considered separate property.

It gets more complicated, though, when the value of separate property is enhanced through community effort. If your husband's earnings—or yours, in a community property state—paid for the $10,000 kitchen remodeling on the summer cottage that was your separate property *before* your marriage, is the value of the entire house still your separate property *after* your marriage? Not likely. Do check with your attorney if you find yourself in this or a similar situation.

It's important to note that any gifts made specifically to you during your marriage are still considered separate property, including inheritances. So if your aunt Minnie left you her classic 1935 roadster, it's yours to keep forever. And anything that you acquired after you were permanently separated from your husband is also considered separate property, including cash gifts from your family that help support you during the separation.

Equitable Distribution

The remaining forty states are governed by "equitable distribution of property" laws. In these states, any assets and earnings that you both have are divided "fairly." In general, this means that about one-half to two-thirds will go to the higher wage earner—in most cases, the husband. Kind of a skewed definition of "fair," wouldn't you say?

There are some similarities between community property states and equitable distribution states. In the case of "fault," the person guilty of committing the fault can receive less that he would otherwise be entitled to in an equitable distribution state. You'll remember that the same is true in a community property state. Likewise, in equitable distribution states, you can claim separate property if you bought or received the property before you got married. And any gifts made specifically to you during the marriage, including inheritances, are also considered separate property.

There are several facts that you should bear in mind if you're filing for divorce in an equitable distribution state. First, it doesn't matter who holds title to the assets you'll be dividing. Property can be in your husband's name, your name, or even a company name, and it will still be considered marital property. (Of course, the key to having an equal share in the property is proving that it exists, particularly if your husband has possession of it or is hiding it.)

An important thing to remember and an important distinction in equitable distribution law is that if your husband owns his own business, that business is considered part of marital property. But if he is not self-employed, then his job and his earning power may be considered his *separate* property. But don't discount his income completely because although it can't be divided per se, it can help determine the amount of alimony you'll receive.

When you file for divorce in an equitable distribution state, you or your husband have sixty or ninety days (depending on the state) to file a net worth statement, listing all marital and non-marital assets and liabilities. Once the papers have been filed, you'll be entitled to equitable distribution, and nothing your husband says or does from that point on can change that.

Separating Yours, Mine, and Ours

Now that you have a working knowledge of the laws that govern property distribution, you can get down to brass tacks. You now have the tools to figure out what you own jointly and what is considered separate property in your state.

Start by taking out the preliminary list of assets you made during the Decision stage. Your list will include marital and non-marital assets. Even if you bought something and its value has declined or dissipated entirely (an interest in a hog farm where all the hogs died, for example), include it on your list. For every asset that you own, try to list when you bought it, to the best of your memory. Is it a high-interest Treasury bond you've held on to for fifteen years and is about to mature? Is it a painting that has gone up in value appreciably since you bought it at a silent auction back in the seventies?

Also, list what you paid for each asset you own and what the approximate current market value is—that is, how much you'd realistically get if you sold it today. This goes for negotiable instruments like stocks and bonds as well as tangible assets like computers and cars. Negotiable instruments are generally much easier to value because there are established markets for selling these assets. Your broker can tell you exactly what most stocks and bonds are worth in today's market. Tangible assets can be much more difficult to value. You can ask an auction house, for example, to value your painting, but its actual worth will be determined by how much a buyer is willing to pay for it.

Make a note of any assets that have increased in value since you bought them. Current valuations may change over the course of your settlement discussions—stock and bond prices can change daily and even hourly—but if you can get an accurate estimate now, it will help you begin dividing your property thoughtfully and intelligently.

Next, write down where you got the money to pay for each asset that you now own. Did you use part of an inheritance that either you or your husband received? Did you take out a bank loan? If so, do you still owe money on the loan?

For major assets like your house, figure out approximately how much your capital gain (your profit) would be if you sold it today and how much tax you'd have to pay on the profit. Generally speaking, the amount of money you've made (the difference between the sale price and the purchase price) is called your tax basis, which determines how much tax you'll have to pay. The computation is actually a bit more involved and it can get pretty confusing, so don't hesitate to enlist the help of your "A team" accountant here.

For any bank accounts that you own, list the account number, the current balance, and the interest rate that you're currently receiving. If it's a time deposit, like a CD, also note the maturity date.

Finally, write down where each asset actually is. Did your husband move out and take his car as well as some of the den furniture along with him? Do you have jewelry or savings bonds in a safety deposit box? Are your savings accounts all at the same bank? It makes sense to identify where each asset is located, not just for your own peace of mind but also in case your lawyer wants to request inspections at a later date.

For certain assets you should definitely consider hiring an appraiser to make sure that you get an accurate estimate of value in writing. Assets that you may need to have appraised could reasonably include any residential or commercial property that you own, whether it's the house you live in, a condominium you rent out, or an office building located in another state. Artwork and antiques with significant value, jewelry, collectibles, period furniture, and rare carpets are other assets likely to require professional appraisal.

The same goes for "paper" assets, such as bank accounts, stocks, bonds, money market funds, mutual funds, and so on. If you call or write to your banker and broker, you can easily get an estimate in writing of your assets' value as of the date of your separation.

When valuing your husband's business, you should strongly consider looking beyond the estimate he gives your lawyer during discovery. If I were you, I sure wouldn't bet the farm that it's an accurate number. (More about this in Part III.) Plan on hiring an expert appraiser to put a value on the business. And don't forget to tell the appraiser everything that you know about your husband's business—and your part, if any, in its operation. If you contributed by keeping financial books, typing correspondence, collecting receivables, or lending a hand in any other way, be sure to include this information. It may not affect the actual appraisal value, but it may very well affect your share of the property settlement. If you helped, it counts. Depending on how much you helped, it can count big time.

What You Owe: Liabilities

You should use the same method for listing liabilities as you did for listing assets. The only major difference is that the "value" of your liabilities is much easier to calculate. The exact amount will be on every mortgage payment, car payment, or credit card statement, and any lender can tell you exactly what you owe. Start by making a list of your outstanding loans, noting the date on which you borrowed the money and whom you need to repay. For each loan that you took out, write down the collateral used to obtain the loan—an equity line of credit on your home, for example. Then write down the interest rate that you're paying, what your monthly payments are, and how long it will take you to repay the loan in full.

Your most substantial liabilities are likely to include the outstanding balance on your home mortgage and other debts to banks or other lending institutions. Any student loans or money that you borrowed to set up a business or professional practice should be on your list as well. And don't forget to include any personal debts to friends or relatives and, of course, any outstanding balances on your credit cards.

Is there an upcoming balloon payment due on your mortgage? If you leased a car with little or no money down, will you owe a large payment at the end of the lease if you opt to buy the car rather than return it to the leasing company? Remember to factor in these and other future principal payments as well.

Finally, calculate how much money it will take to repay all of your loans in full. Once you've done so, you and your husband will be able to split up your debts, just as you're splitting up your assets.

"Don't Ask, Don't Tell"

So far I've talked about the assets and liabilities that are out there in the open, clearly visible to the naked eye. But what if you suspect that there's more to your joint property than meets the eye? What if you have a gut feeling that closer examination under a fine-tuned financial microscope may tell a different story altogether?

Better to leave no stone unturned. Many women are astonished at what they find hidden under some very unlikely rocks.

When President Clinton was considering whether his famous (or infamous) "don't ask, don't tell" policy would work in the military, he could have gained ample insight by looking no further than the nearest marriage. It's mind-boggling how many married women have little or no say in handling their family finances. Some don't even know exactly how much their husbands earn, and they certainly don't know about hidden assets their husbands may have secreted somewhere.

If women are kept in the dark about the family finances even when they're happily married, how will they know if they're getting their fair share during a divorce?

Annie, now in her late fifties, was brought up believing that "you just don't ask"—even about how much money her husband, Ray, was earning as an orthopedic surgeon. She didn't want him to think that she was judging him by his bank account or that she didn't trust him to manage the family's financial affairs. He paid all the major household bills at his office and deposited funds into a joint checking account for everyday expenses. Annie spent the money; Ray balanced the checkbook.

During her divorce proceedings, when it came time to divide up the assets of their thirty-year marriage, Annie was completely in the dark. And, amazingly, she still had the same "don't ask, don't tell" attitude toward her husband and any discussion of money. She still didn't want to rock the financial boat. She just wanted to make things easier on everyone. Needless to say, Annie was an accident waiting to happen.

Her wish to keep things amicable and to smooth over troubled waters typifies the attitude of many divorcing women. Unfortunately, many women like Annie don't know the value of family assets and are completely unfamiliar with the family finances. This is clearly a distinct disadvantage when it comes time to negotiate a settlement agreement. But it doesn't have to spell gloom and doom for divorcing women. It just means that you'll have to work a little harder and dig a little deeper to get anything even remotely resembling a fair shake.

Searching for Buried Treasure

What if you've always been completely out of the loop when it comes to the family finances? How do you know that what you see is what you get?

Frankly, you don't. And this is where things can get sticky. I'm certainly not implying that all men siphon off part of their income or keep investments hidden from their wives. But some do. If you have any reason at all to suspect this may be the case in your marriage, it's better to do a little detective work than to deny the possibility. How do you know for sure? Again, you don't. Most of the time there's no smoking gun, no handwriting on the wall. But better to be super-safe and financially secure than completely clueless and sorry forever after. None of us wants to believe our husbands are capable of keeping private "buried treasure" behind our backs or even under our very noses. But, sadly, it does happen, and avoiding the truth doesn't help.

There are many reasons why men divert funds away from joint accounts. Sometimes *he's* afraid of getting left. If he feels as though the two of you have been growing apart for some time, he might want to put a little something away for the future—his future. Or he may feel that having a secret "stash" gives him power—a way of being in control and asserting his dominance in the relationship. Or, forgive me for saying this, but he may just be a dishonest creep.

Whatever the reason, if you suspect that your husband has been hiding assets, you're going to need to start searching for them ASAP. You may be able to do a fair amount of Sherlock Holmes (or Nancy Drew) work by yourself before calling in your "A team." If you find a paper trail of evidence showing that hidden assets do exist but you can't locate them, you or your lawyer can hire a professional investigator or a forensic accountant whose job it is to ferret out those hidden assets. But as always, doing as much as you can yourself will help keep your costs to a minimum.

When you begin your search, start by revisiting the list of assets you put together earlier detailing your unhidden assets, including their location. Make sure every asset you can think of is on that list, whether it's in your name alone or in both your names. Think about stocks that you've bought, jewelry, furniture, and even frequent flier miles you've accrued and never used. If it's not on your list and you can't account for it, but you know for a fact that you own it, where is it?

Remember that while each state has different laws governing marital property, generally speaking, all money and assets acquired during your marriage belong to both of you. And even if some of these assets have been hidden from you, you have legal recourse in demanding that they be divided equally between you. But first, of course, you have to find them. Hidden assets are usually hidden because they're worth big bucks, so it's certainly in your financial interest to uncover them. Go to it!

Digging Deeper

Assets can be hidden in very creative ways, so you'll need to be very creative in your search for them.

Hidden assets can also take many forms, but a common one is owning real estate under someone else's name. You'd be surprised how a few well-placed, innocent-sounding questions can lead to an out-of-state apartment building held in your brother-in-law's name but actually paid for by your husband.

Your antennae should also go up if your husband ever asked you to sign a business loan or an application for a second mortgage. If you signed on the dotted line and didn't think any more about it, you also probably didn't think about where that loan money was going—possibly into a bank account that you never knew existed. It could be in an out-of-state account or in an investment that your husband never told you about.

If your husband owns his own business, he may list employees on his payroll that don't actually work for him. They may not even exist at all. He could be cashing their paychecks himself and keeping the money out of your reach.

And unbeknownst to you, your husband might have cashed in his insurance policy or he might have borrowed funds from his pension plan, investing the proceeds elsewhere. This can be the most devastating betrayal of trust because most women regard life insurance and pension assets as "ultrasafe" money—virtually sacrosanct and untouchable.

Following the Paper Trail

As you follow the paper trail, you may find all sorts of receipts, telephone bills, business papers, and—if you're lucky—bank and brokerage account confirmations. Even a seemingly innocuous slip of paper fished from the trash might lead you to a hidden bank, brokerage, or credit card account. Check the numbers on anything you find against numbers from accounts you already know about.

Also, feel free to ask your husband about anything you don't understand, but be sure not to tip your hand or voice your suspicions out loud. Avoid grilling him or taking a heavy-handed approach. A Columbo-like "by the way" query is much more likely to get you good results here.

When you speak to your husband, jot down notes as soon as possible after your conversation. He may tell you about certain assets and deny their existence later on. If you have no proof that they ever existed, you may have no recourse. But if, as a result of your conversation with him, you can prove that there's something worth searching for, your lawyer can help you find it.

Think about whether your husband has taken a lot of business trips to the same location, either out of state or out of the country. Consider the possibility that he may be "visiting" bank accounts elsewhere.

And if you come across any unfamiliar keys, try to find out what they open—even if you're concerned that they'll open a door you'd rather not walk through. They could just be for run-of-the-mill file cabinets at his office, but don't rule out the possibility of safety deposit boxes, other offices, or even other homes.

If your husband keeps business records at home, make copies of everything you can. These will help you later if there's any dispute over how much money his business is actually worth.

Finally, use your common sense. Think back to anything that may have sounded even vaguely suspicious. Did your husband ever tell you that he made a bad stock investment or that he lost money in real estate that you didn't even know he owned? Try to remember the details. If it sounded strange to you at the time, it should set off early warning signals now.

Snoopy or Charlie Brown?

If copying papers and searching for evidence feels too much like snooping, remember that if he's done nothing wrong, you have nothing to worry about. Don't get overly paranoid. Just don't be too naive, either. Again, better safe than sorry.

Above all, you should stay within your comfort level even if it means taking a less vigilant approach to hunting for hidden assets. You need to weigh your feelings against what even the most expert attorney or accountant might advise. If you feel strongly that your husband hasn't hidden any assets and that conducting an invasive search might antagonize him and jeopardize your chances of getting the settlement that you really want, go with your instincts. Make sure that your "A team" understands the parameters of your comfort zone and respects your desire to stay within it.

Personally, though, I'd rather feel like Snoopy than Charlie

Brown, that too-trusting blockhead who keeps getting the ball pulled out from under him, landing him flat on his butt time after time.

Think about it.

Keeping an Eye on the Bottom Line

Whether it's assets you know about or hidden assets you've managed to uncover, always keep an eye on the bottom line. Protect what belongs to you, especially in the case of major assets like your home, your car, and your investment portfolio. Early on in the divorce proceedings, you should check the title on any property that you own. For real estate holdings, contact a title company or go to your county recorder's office and search for the deed to your property to see how the title reads. With regard to your car, your investments, and *any* joint accounts, it's very important to make sure that your name does not get removed before the property is formally divided. Communicate in writing with stockbrokers, bankers, and the Department of Motor Vehicles to request that your name be kept on anything you hold jointly until your divorce is finalized (unless you have been advised otherwise by your lawyer). This will clear up any confusion over who owns what and will protect you against at least one divorce dirty trick that some husbands try to get away with. There are many more, but you can avoid them if you know what to look for.

Be on the Lookout for These Divorce Dirty Tricks

Even at this early stage in the divorce process, there are plenty of dirty tricks to watch out for. This is the time when you may feel held hostage by your emotions and willing to do anything to stop the onslaught of negative feelings. But this is not the time to start giving in left and right to your husband's every demand du jour. In fact, if you keep your head together now, it will pave the way for even more clearheadedness later on.

Don't let your husband manipulate your emotions or take advantage of the vulnerability that you may be feeling, using it to his financial gain and to your detriment. It may be a calculated effort on his part, but then again, he may *not* be doing it on purpose with the intention of hurting you. It could just be a reflection of the way he's used to taking a tough stand in business: "Business is business. No hard feelings. Nothing personal." But the impact on you could be very personal and quite enough to send your emotions into another tailspin. In fact, you may have moments when you'd agree to almost anything just to get him off your back. Don't do it!

Don't make any decisions out of a misguided sense of guilt, either. Maybe you still haven't sorted out what went wrong in your marriage and are still vulnerable to the suggestion that, even if he left you, it's somehow all your fault (which it probably isn't). Or you may have initiated the breakup and are feeling responsible for hurting other people. Either way, think hard before shouldering all the blame. And don't get talked into making financial "amends" for causing others emotional pain—real or perceived.

Other dirty tricks take advantage of the fact that divorce is expensive.

Your husband may refuse to agree to even your most reasonable requests, hoping that you'll run up a huge legal bill and be forced to cave in to his demands rather than risk incurring even higher fees.

And if your husband has deeper pockets than you do, he may try to wear you down by waiting until you've depleted your money supply and have nowhere else to turn—except, of course, to him. At this point he's likely to attach all kinds of conditions to lending you financial support. Don't give in.

My client Tania called me in tears one day not too long ago, requesting that a credit card be issued on her brokerage account immediately. "No problem," I said, "but why are you crying?"

"Because I've never been so humiliated in my life," she replied. "I was at Robinsons trying to pay for a baby gift for my granddaughter, and the salesperson said that my credit card had been canceled. She cut it up right in front of me! Can you believe that my husband just moved out of the house and has already canceled my credit cards without even telling me?"

I do believe it. And *you'd* better believe that there are plenty more divorce dirty tricks that you need to be on the lookout for. Here are just some of the doozies that I've heard over the years:

- The electric company turns off your power because your husband hasn't paid the bill for the last three months even though you both agree that it's his responsibility.
- Your husband funnels all your savings into his own account two days before he files for divorce, leaving you broke.
- Your husband asks his boss to withhold part of his salary or commission until after the divorce, making his income appear lower so you get less than you're entitled to.
- You find out that your husband's many business trips to the Caribbean were actually visits to an offshore bank account that you knew nothing about.
- You discover that your husband has generously "gifted" some of your joint assets to his friends and relatives so the assets can't be split in the property settlement. (You can be sure the "gifts" will be returned to him soon after the divorce is final.)
- Knowing that you'd like to keep the house after the divorce, your husband sells you his share, conveniently forgetting to mention that he'll be pocketing tax-free money while you'll likely end up with a hefty tax bill should you decide to sell the house at a later date.
- To your husband's "amazement," his "almost worthless" stock options suddenly become worth a bundle when his pri-

vately held company goes public six months after your divorce. He gets a bundle; you get zip.

- And the most insidious dirty trick of all: Your husband uses your children as emotional yo-yos in an attempt to undermine your resolve (to say nothing of your morale) and force you to give in to his settlement demands. This, in my opinion, is manipulation at its worst—the lowest of the low.

Once you've managed to steel yourself against these and other tricks that your husband may try to slip past you, it's time to turn your attention to protecting yourself from the rest of life's hazards.

Insuring Your Well-being

It doesn't take a rocket scientist these days to know that insurance coverage is critical—and costly. Before you go any further, dig up copies of any insurance policies that you already have. Pay close attention to where you're covered, where you're not, and when the policies expire. Here's where a little footwork today can save you major money down the road.

Your Health Checkup

Find out if you and your children are included on a group policy through your place of business or your husband's. If not, it's likely you have an individual plan. If you do have an individual plan, check to see how much your deductible is and, if you continue with the same coverage, what your premiums will be for the next six months, for the next year, and beyond. If your children *are* covered on your husband's medical plan, try to negotiate for him to continue providing coverage for them until they are at least eighteen years old. Be sure to include this in writing in your final settlement agreement later on.

If you're currently covered by your husband's group policy, notify the person who handles insurance and employee benefits at his company that you're getting divorced. If the company employs at least twenty people, you will receive information about COBRA, the Consolidated Omnibus Budget Reform Act, which entitles you to a continuation of your health coverage for a maximum of thirty-six months. You'll have sixty days to decide whether you want to stay on your husband's policy. Bear in mind, though, that instead of being a co-pay plan (where you pay part of the premium and the employer pays the rest), COBRA requires you to pay the full amount yourself. If you opt for this coverage under COBRA, don't forget to start looking for the coverage you'll need after the thirty-six months are up. Another caveat: If you remarry during the thirty-six-month period or take a job that provides health coverage, you may no longer be eligible for coverage under COBRA.

One avenue to pursue may be your own place of business. If your company offers group health insurance coverage and you've never taken advantage of it in the past, now is the time to find out how much it will cost for the same kind of coverage you have now. Some women who can get insurance through their own places of business have opted to go through their husbands' companies instead because the premiums were lower. Often, you can switch over and keep the same doctors. If your company offers coverage by an HMO, you may also have access to a co-pay plan. With a health maintenance organization (HMO) you'll have no deductible and only a small cost per visit. Sometimes it makes better financial sense to go this route unless you absolutely prefer seeing a doctor who is in private practice. Of course, with the advent of health care reform, it's entirely possible that in the future this decision will be a moot point.

Disability Coverage

Disability insurance basically guarantees that you will continue to receive a certain percentage of your income should you become disabled and unable to work. If you are counting on your income as a primary means of support, disability insurance is a must. It is usually available as part of your health coverage for an extra charge and is well worth the cost—especially if you have children to provide for.

Your Life and Your Husband's

Most likely, any insurance that you carry on your own life currently names your husband as primary beneficiary. Your immediate emotional response may be to take his name off the policy before sunset. But logic may dictate a different course of action. What if you die before your children turn eighteen, leaving your husband with sole financial responsibility for raising them? Regardless of who gets custody in your settlement, if your husband ends up taking care of your children alone, he may need the lump sum of cash from your life insurance policy to provide for them adequately. If this isn't an issue for you, that's fine. But if it is, remember to swallow your pride and do what's in your children's best long-term interest even if it sticks in your throat at the moment.

Also be aware of the fact that if you name your children as primary beneficiaries and you die before they reach age eighteen, the insurance proceeds may be retained by the insurance company until the children turn eighteen. Alternatively, the insurance company may require the court to appoint a guardian, which can be a costly and complicated process. Another big problem with this option is that when your kids do turn eighteen, they will receive all the money in one lump sum. This can be pretty overwhelming for the average eighteen-year-old, so unless you're absolutely confident that your children can handle it, you may elect not to choose this option, especially if substantial dollars are involved.

You also need to consider your husband's life insurance coverage. It's obviously in your best interest to remain as beneficiary on his policy. Aside from the childcare issues discussed earlier, there's another clear benefit to you: If you're likely to receive alimony as part of your settlement, you can virtually "insure" continuing support even beyond his death by remaining as beneficiary. If your husband dies prematurely, the insurance proceeds will provide you with the financial resources that you need to live on and to raise your children. If he's amenable, this is clearly the way to go.

So far, so good. You've negotiated or filed for temporary alimony and child support, and by now you probably have a pretty good handle on your assets and liabilities. You have also managed, I hope, to avoid the worst of the divorce dirty tricks.

If you feel as if you've made about a gazillion plans and a bazillion lists during the Planning Period, you're probably right. But hang in there. I can't promise that it won't get worse before it gets better, but it *will* get better.

PART III

•••

The Big Picture

Looking Back but Moving Ahead

● ● ●

The Big Picture period of your divorce may be the first time you've had a chance to take a good, deep breath in months. And it may be your first real opportunity to come to terms with the fact that your divorce is going forward, that it's really and truly happening. Emotionally, you may be looking to the future while a big chunk of your heart is still living in the past. But while you're still forced to spend many hours with lawyers and accountants, you are starting to see the light at the end of the tunnel.

Now that things are moving along, it's all really hitting you, isn't it? You may start wondering again (perhaps for the three thousandth time) if you made the right decision or if your husband has really thought about what he's doing. Every so often you may be convinced that this is all just one big mistake. But overriding that feeling may be the sense that something better is in sight, that, in fact, the best is yet to come.

Soon you will begin building your new life. The divorce that now seems like a huge mountain almost impossible to climb will later be only one of many blips on your life's horizon. Okay, so maybe it will be a big blob, but it will be a blob that's behind you.

The Big Picture phase is about looking at the whole enchilada and carefully analyzing all the documents you've gathered in preparation for negotiating a moneysmart settlement. It includes calculating the value of your assets (and liabilities) and thinking about how you'd like to divide them. It's about negotiating for alimony and child support. And it's about understanding what's really at stake when you draft your final settlement agreement. The assets you're looking at now are the biggies: the business one or both of you owns, your home, your savings and investment accounts, and your retirement plans. Getting an accurate valuation of these assets is critical before you begin negotiating your settlement. As I mentioned in Part II, some assets are harder to value than others and will likely require the help of a professional appraiser. Even though some of the calculating and sorting out can be a supremely tedious task, it's definitely worth the effort, so hang in there. The Big Picture is an important stage of your divorce process, and the sooner you get through it, the sooner you'll be on your way to the better life that lies ahead.

Who Owns What? Your Business Assets

The easiest way to get started is to deal with the businesses owned by you, your husband, or both of you together. This doesn't mean that you need to own Bloomingdale's for it to count as a business asset. Law, dental, and medical practices are all businesses. Likewise, any store or company, from a Dunkin' Donuts franchise to a mom-and-pop fix-it shop. Whatever the business is, it has present and future value that needs to be assessed before you draft your settlement.

In Part II you listed the business as one of your assets and documented your contribution to it, whether you were the president or the unpaid bookkeeper. Whether it's you or your husband who owns the business, now is when you need to decide how to divide it after the divorce. How will you do this? It's usually best to hire a professional business appraiser who can look at the equipment, at the amount of income the business generates, and at the business's performance over time in order to determine its worth. So if you don't have one already lined up, plan on adding an appraiser to your "A team" pronto.

Different states have different yardsticks when it comes to determining who owns how much of the business. Community property, common law, or equitable distribution considerations govern how the business gets divided. Past contributions are also factored in—both financial and non-financial.

Who put up the money to buy it in the first place? And who made it all happen from the get-go? Let's say you waitressed at the House of Pancakes for three years to pay the bills while your husband was in law school. Even if that happened light years ago, you may still have a stake in his law practice today—and tomorrow, depending where you live. Some states consider a professional degree marital property; other states consider the professional license but not the degree itself marital property. Still other states (California, for example) will reimburse you if you supported your husband through school. So, all things considered, maybe all those years of shlepping blueberry short stacks and maple syrup weren't wasted after all!

If you live in a state where professional, graduate, or trade school degrees are considered marital property, that *doesn't* mean you get to keep your husband's practice when you divide the assets, but it does mean you'll be entitled to some of the rewards of the practice, which you'll likely receive in the form of other assets. So while your husband may get to keep his law practice and all future proceeds from it, you may get a greater share of the house or higher alimony payments in return.

What's the Business Worth?

The issue of valuing assets can be anything but clear-cut. Assume you'll have to prove the value of anything important enough to consider dividing. And even if this means hiring a qualified—and expensive—expert to assess the value of what you own, it's well worth the cost. *Don't* try to do it yourself here, especially if it comes to putting a dollar figure on your husband's practice or business which may include intangible assets that are much harder to value than, say, a portfolio of stocks. Things like name recognition and goodwill definitely add to the value of a business, but they can be hard to quantify. It pays to have a professional opinion, so don't try to save money now at the risk of an undervaluation that will end up costing you much more later on.

Before you hire an appraiser, you'll want to think about whether you and your husband can arrive at a mutually agreed upon value for the business on your own. Frankly, the chances of this happening are usually slim to none. Sometimes the numbers don't leave much room for interpretation, though, especially if you have just paid taxes or have recently applied for a business loan. (I'm assuming, of course, that you've valued your business fairly and paid your taxes honestly as all good citizens do.)

If you do agree on a value, you can save money by not hiring an appraiser. But if you don't agree, consider it money well spent making sure you get a fair valuation so you can get a fair share of the business.

Are Two Heads Better Than One?

You and your husband can use the same appraiser, or you can each hire a different one. Using the same appraiser obviously means spending less money and maybe having fewer fights, but it works only if the appraiser is completely unbiased.

Using two different appraisers may make you feel more secure about getting an impartial opinion and will certainly give you one less situation in which you have to deal directly with your husband. But what if the two appraisers disagree on a value? Then you can be in a real pickle.

Best case: You and your husband agree to split the difference. Worst case: You can't agree, and you end up going to court. Preparing for a trial will cost you bongo bucks in the long run, not to mention a lot of aggravation and emotional wear and tear, so my advice is to try using the same appraiser—at least at first. Make sure it's someone whom both attorneys know and respect. If the appraiser is honest, fair, and knows the business, you could save yourself a lot of money and potential hassle by going this route.

Bear in mind, though, that using the same appraiser will work to your benefit only if your husband is being completely open and aboveboard about his business interests. If he willingly makes available his records and all other financial information, you'll be in good shape. If he resists or if you have reason to believe that he's hiding assets, you're in for trouble, so consult your lawyer immediately.

The Business Bottom Line

If all goes well, once the appraisal is completed you'll get a report outlining how the value of the business was calculated and how the final numbers stack up.

You'll then be ready to figure out how to divide this asset. Depending on whether you own the business jointly or whether only one of you owns it—and, of course, depending on which state you live in—you'll be entitled to a certain share of the business. How do you actually receive your share? One way is to sell the business and divide the proceeds. This method isn't used very often. More commonly, the person who owns the business will keep it in exchange for other assets.

Here is where you might want to negotiate to keep the family home in exchange for your husband's keeping the business. Likewise, if there are other assets you feel strongly about keeping, now is the time to put them on the table for discussion.

Your House: Love It or Leave It

The house may be the most difficult asset to deal with for several reasons. For many families it is the single most valuable asset they own. The house may also be the asset that has appreciated the most in value; thus, selling it will incur the greatest potential tax liability. And, of course, the house usually has the strongest emotional tie—it's the place where your kids took their first steps, lost their baby teeth, did cartwheels on the front lawn. Leaving those memories behind isn't easy.

What to Do? What to Do?

So you have this valuable asset and you have to figure out what to do with it. Will you sell it and divide the proceeds? If you don't sell it, who gets it? And what does the other person get instead?

Your options are pretty well defined. One of you can choose to keep the house in exchange for other assets—for example, the family business or a well-funded retirement plan. If you decide to sell the house, you can do so now and divide the proceeds immediately, or you can plan on selling it later and dividing the proceeds at that time. Some couples choose to delay selling their house in the hope of getting a higher price at some future date. With some real estate markets in different parts of the country still severely depressed (California, for example), this strategy may make sense.

What you do and when you do it is up to you. But before you decide what's best for you, talk to your "A team"—especially your accountant—so you can factor in the tax ramifications of your different options. Also think seriously about the cash or other assets that you may be giving up in order to keep the house. Apply the Two C's (common sense and comfort level) and figure out what's most important to you.

Crunch the Numbers

Here's how to make a commonsense, moneysmart decision about whether to keep or sell your house. Before you do anything else, figure out how much the house is worth. What would you get if you sold it today? Don't guess. Talk to a knowledgeable real estate professional who will base her estimate of your house's value on comparable homes in your area, factoring in improvements you've made since you bought it or any repairs that need to be made. Also consider how much equity you have in the house: Is it mortgaged to the hilt, or are you almost finished paying off your loan? Don't make the mistake of assuming that if your house is worth $250,000, you'll get that much when you sell. If it's a buyer's market, you may have to settle for less than your asking price. And don't forget the cost of selling the house, including the potentially hefty taxes that you'll owe. Net, net—you'll likely end up with a lot less than $250,000 in your pocket.

If you and your husband sell the house jointly—whether now or later—you'll split the tax liability. But if you keep the house as part of your settlement and sell it at some point after the divorce, the tax bite will be all yours. How painful will it be? It can hurt plenty if you bought your house twenty or thirty years ago when prices were appreciably lower than they are today. But if you bought your house in the late 1980s when the real estate market was very pricey in most parts of the country, you may not owe the taxman all that much when you sell. Of course, the only way that happens is if you don't make much of a profit or if you—God forbid—sell at a loss. So not having to pay taxes can be a double-edged sword.

If you and your husband are talking seriously about selling the house and dividing the proceeds immediately, there are important tax repercussions you should consider. Depending on your age, it may make a lot more sense purely from a tax standpoint to wait a few years, owing to a specific provision in the tax law. An exemption in the tax code states that if you're over fifty-five, you can take a onetime exclusion on $125,000 of your profit. That means you don't have to pay taxes if the profit on the sale of your house is $125,000 or less; if it's more, you pay taxes only on the amount of profit above $125,000. Good deal, wouldn't you say?

And here's what may be another good deal: If you sell your house at a profit and buy another house of greater or equal value to the one you sold within two years, you will *not* have to pay taxes on the sale of house number one. This applies regardless of your age. The problem is that most divorcing women trade down, not up, when they sell their house, so this tax provision may sound good on paper but may not be much help in real life.

Don't Move Away from Your Comfort Zone . . .

We've talked about some of the financial realities involved in deciding whether to keep or sell the family home. Now let's consider the emotional realities that are so much a part of this decision.

For some women, even if it doesn't make terrific financial sense, moving to a new place seems like a great way to start with a clean slate. "I just can't handle the thought of living in that house and walking from room to room remembering the past," says forty-seven-year-old Meg who divorced last January. "Believe me, it's not nostalgia for the good times, either. Don't get me wrong. I love the house. It's a forty-year-old colonial with so much charm and grace that the thought of selling it truly makes me want to cry. What I really can't stand, though, is remembering the fights over breakfast at the kitchen table almost every single morning. No thanks, I can live without those scenes playing in my head over and over again every time I want a cup of coffee. As much as I love the house, I really need to be somewhere else."

My client Debbie disagrees. "Well, obviously it's not easy for me to sleep alone in the bed that Chuck and I shared for almost twelve years. And I can't even vaguely deal with the idea of sleeping with anyone else—at least not yet, not after only ten months," she says. "But staying here is the right thing to do for my kids. They turned their first somersaults on our front lawn and saw a baby bird for the first time nesting in the old oak tree in our backyard. They *need* the memories; they need the stability of being in the house they grew up in and the next-door neighbor kids they've known forever. Truthfully, I feel like I don't really have a choice."

But Debbie *does* have a choice. In her case, her choice is to put her children's needs (or at least her perception of their needs) before her own. If that works for her, fine. Your choice may be entirely different from hers, and that's fine, too. There isn't a right or wrong answer, and this isn't about being selfish or selfless. It's about making decisions that feel right to you.

It's a pretty good bet that you will feel more attached to your house than, say, a municipal bond or a stock portfolio. How can you take something with such a strong emotional pull and think of it dispassionately as just another asset? By not losing sight of your common sense.

... But Don't Leave Your Common Sense Behind

Let's say that after thinking about what you want to do and considering what's best for everyone concerned, you decide keeping the house feels right to you. Now let's inject a little financial reality so you can be as moneysmart as possible in making this decision. First of all, make sure that you can afford to live in the house if you do get to keep it. Can you make the mortgage payments, heat it in the winter, repair whatever needs repairing, and still afford to pay property taxes twice a year? If not, where's the money going to come from? Your parents? Your husband? Heaven?

I don't have enough fingers and toes to count the number of women I know who don't think these things through from a financial perspective until it's too late and they're sitting on a pile of unpaid bills. "Who figured it would be such a cold winter?" says Deanie, a bone-weary forty-one-year-old mother of three who works part-time as a medical technician. "I sure underestimated my utility bill, and I sure didn't figure on having to replace half the shingles on the roof this year. I don't know how I'm going to pay for all this," she says with a sigh.

The moral of the story is to consider both realities—emotional *and* financial—when you decide whether to keep your house or sell it. Factor in *both* when you value your home during the negotiation proceedings. Don't let your heart rule your head.

And don't forget to allow for price fluctuations—and a possible downturn—in the real estate market. This isn't rocket science, it's common sense. But you'd be amazed at how often common sense gets lost in the emotional shuffle. Always think of today's appraisals and negotiations as tomorrow's chance at a financially secure future. Part of thinking about this future also includes thinking about your retirement years and how to plan for them, whether they're five years away or twenty-five years away.

Retirement Assets

No matter what age you are, retirement will play two key roles in your divorce. First, in community property states, retirement benefits, including pension plans and social security payments, are considered property that you and your husband share. Second, a major financial priority in achieving a moneysmart divorce settlement *must* be planning for your own retirement.

Let me say from the outset that the following discussion about retirement planning may not be scintillating reading, but keep your eyes open. Your future depends on it.

What Is a Retirement Plan?

Retirement plans can be tax deductible, tax deferred, or both. When the plan is tax deductible, the money you or your husband contributes each year actually reduces your taxes for that year. Tax deferral is different. As the word implies, deferral means you are deferring or putting off paying taxes on income or capital gains in your retirement portfolio. Some retirement plans are "twofers," both tax deductible and tax deferred. This means you get to take a tax deduction on the amount of your contribution every year *and* you get to wait until you withdraw funds (when your tax bracket may be lower) to pay ordinary income tax on your portfolio's principal, income earnings, and capital gains. Be careful about withdrawing funds from retirement plans before age 59½, though. You'll face a stiff 10 percent penalty if you do, with very few exceptions.

Some retirement plans are only tax deferred and not tax deductible; for example, some people can no longer deduct IRA contributions. Annuities (which can be an addendum to your retirement plan) are tax deferred but not tax deductible. (IRAs and annuities are explained on the following pages.)

Is a Retirement Plan the Same as an Investment?

Strictly speaking, no. Retirement plans are *not* in and of themselves specific investments. IRAs, Keoghs, 401(k)s, and other retirement plans are merely vehicles, or "umbrellas," offering a wide range of investment choices that can include mutual funds, stocks, bonds, CDs, money markets—almost any kind of investment you want. This is important to remember. When you evaluate your retirement plan (and your husband's) during the divorce process, what you are really evaluating are the specific investments within the plans to assess their value and their appropriateness for you.

What Is an IRA?

An IRA is an individual retirement account. It's a type of retirement plan available to any worker under age 70½. You can contribute up to $2,000 a year, which may be fully, partially, or not at all tax deductible. If you and your husband both work, you can each contribute $2,000. If you don't work, your husband can establish his own $2,000 IRA and a spousal IRA with an additional contribution of up to $250 for you. (Theoretically, the $2,250 can be allocated equally between the two IRAs, but I've never seen this happen in real life.)

This is one area where you may have gotten shortchanged during your marriage, especially if you didn't work outside the home. With your husband putting away fully eight times as much per year in his IRA as you likely contributed to yours, there's bound to be a substantial discrepancy in the value of your two accounts.

One silver lining, though: When you begin receiving temporary alimony—even during your separation—you can count this as income, which will allow you to contribute up to $2,000 to your IRA even if you don't work outside the home.

Depending on whether you *are* working and the dollar amount of the temporary support you receive, you may or may not be able to deduct the IRA. But because your money will grow tax deferred under the IRA umbrella, you may want to make the contribution even if you can't take the deduction. If putting away the $2,000 doesn't cause you financial hardship in the short run, I would strongly encourage you to "bank" this money for the long run.

Please note: Changes may be on the horizon because Congress is currently considering several different legislative proposals affecting IRA contributions and deductibility. Check with your "A team" accountant for further information.

The 401(k) Plan

This is a retirement plan typically sponsored by a company, which may or may not be offered in conjunction with another retirement plan. It is essentially a salary-reduction program that allows you to contribute pretax income up to a specific dollar limit each year.

Sometimes a company will match your 401(k) contributions dollar for dollar. This means that if you put away $5,000, your employer will put away an additional $5,000 for you. By matching funds, they are giving you a 100 percent return on your money right from the get-go. Better than pennies from heaven!

With some company retirement plans you have total jurisdiction over the investments in your 401(k), meaning you get to choose exactly what you want to own. In other plans, your investment choices may be limited to a specific number of mutual funds, or you may have to invest at least part of your 401(k) money—usually the employer's matched contribution—in company stock. Be informed. If you have questions, look to the company's human resources director for answers or further direction.

The Keogh Plan

A Keogh is a retirement plan for the self-employed. You can make annual, tax-deductible contributions up to a maximum percentage of your income and to a maximum dollar amount.

If you establish a Keogh, you can have an IRA as well, although your IRA contribution may not be tax deductible. Like an IRA, a Keogh is not a specific investment but a type of retirement plan in which you can own any number of different investments.

SEP-IRAs, Profit Shares, Money Purchase Plans, and Defined Benefit Plans

These are all different types of retirement plans with different and very specific eligibility and reporting requirements and contribution limits. What they have in common is that they are worth only as much as the investments within them are worth. There is no such thing as a good or bad retirement plan, but there definitely are good and bad stocks, bonds, mutual funds, and so forth. Judge each investment on a case-by-case basis.

Annuities

Annuities are tax-deferred investments. An annuity is not actually a retirement plan. Think of an annuity as a *nondeductible* addition to your retirement savings. Like retirement plans, annuity investments are tax deferred, so earnings and capital gains are not subject to current taxation. There are also tax penalties for early withdrawals before age 59 ½.

A fixed-rate annuity is almost like a CD in that it pays a

specific interest rate each year. Variable annuities, on the other hand, are very much like mutual funds. This generally makes them riskier than fixed-rate annuities, but because of their growth potential, they can sometimes prove to be excellent investments.

Annuities are good supplements to retirement plans because there is no limitation on the amount you can invest—unlike the ceilings imposed on retirement plan contributions. If your husband owns an annuity, it can be worth a substantial amount of money, so be sure to check it out.

Evaluate your husband's retirement plans carefully. Be certain to leave no stone unturned. If you assume that your husband has no retirement plan because he's self-employed, you should rethink that assumption posthaste and find out for sure. Talk to the human resources or employee benefits director at his place of business for further information. And do check your tax returns for any deductions taken for retirement plan contributions in current or previous years.

Assessing the Value of Retirement Plan Assets

When you're considering how retirement plan assets will be divided during your divorce settlement, it's critically important to establish as accurate a value as possible for each investment in each retirement plan. Begin by calculating the present value of each plan as well as the estimated future value in the year when you can begin withdrawing funds without incurring a tax penalty. In plain English, figure out what it's worth now and what you can reasonably expect it to be worth at a specific point in the future. In calculating the value of the retirement plans, remember that there is a difference between the legal value of a plan and its financial value.

The legal value is the one recognized by the court. It's the plan's "paper worth" as indicated by an account value included on the bank, brokerage, or mutual fund statements you receive. This applies equally to any type of corporate pension plan, IRA, Keogh, and so forth, and also includes annuities. If your husband has a company-sponsored plan, you can contact the plan administrator for assistance in determining its value.

The financial value of a retirement plan can be very different from its legal value. The financial value is generally lower because it takes into account taxes, fees, or commissions and possible early withdrawal penalties. The financial value is clearly more accurate than the legal value because it represents bottom-line financial reality. If you own two hundred shares of XYZ stock with a current legal value of $4,000, you can be sure that you'll end up with less than $4,000 in your pocket after you net out commission costs to sell the stock and pay taxes if any are due.

What to Consider When Negotiating

If you had your druthers—your best-case perfect settlement from heaven—how would you choose to divide up your retirement plan assets? One of the important points to consider is whether a plan was funded with pretax or after-tax dollars. If taxes have already been paid, think seriously about trying to keep this plan. If taxes have not already been paid, remember that you're the one who'll be paying the piper later. Remember, too, only that portion of any retirement plan accumulated during your marriage can be considered joint property. So if you were the proud owner of a hefty 401(k) plan before your marriage, it's still yours to have and to hold.

There are several other factors to consider when you're deciding how to divvy up your retirement plans: the QDRO (see p. 127), which can act as a financial "guarantee" if your husband refuses to pay alimony or if he dies prematurely; the plan's vesting schedule; and the actual point in time when you can touch and feel the money in the account.

The Qualified Domestic Relations Order (QDRO)

A Qualified Domestic Relations Order (QDRO) is essentially a court order that designates how a specific retirement plan will be divided, to whom it will be paid, and when. The QDRO assigns you the right to receive all or a portion of your husband's benefits under the provisions of his retirement plan. It includes all benefits to which your husband is entitled as of either your separation date or the actual date of your divorce, depending on which you agree to use. It also outlines provisions for survivor's benefits in the event of the plan owner's premature death. QDROs are used most often in the case of a company paying out pension plan proceeds. The court order in effect tells the plan administrators who is entitled to receive the money.

You can sometimes use a QDRO to "insure" yourself against your husband's refusing to pay alimony. Under certain circumstances, the court can include a special provision in your QDRO that entitles you to your ex's pension fund money if he's delinquent in his alimony payments. So while you can't force him to put his alimony check in the mail each month, you may be able to force him to pay up out of his pension plan. A caveat here: You will be able to access these funds immediately only if early distributions are allowed by plan provisions, and you will certainly want to consult with your "A team" accountant regarding potential tax liabilities in doing so.

Your Vested Interest

When you consider any retirement plan belonging to either you or your husband, remember that you are required to work at a company for a minimum number of years before you're entitled to full retirement benefits. This is called vesting. It means if you leave your job before you're entitled to receive full retirement benefits, you may in fact receive nothing at all. Or you may be partially vested, which means you're entitled to receive only a percentage of the full amount. Important point: Some states don't count retirement funds as marital property unless and until they are fully vested.

Bear in mind that even if you or your husband has worked at a company long enough to be fully vested, you may still be shy of retirement age and therefore subject to a 10 percent penalty if funds are withdrawn at this time. If the two of you agree to split the proceeds of one retirement plan by taking an immediate cash distribution, make sure each of you gets a separate check for your share of the proceeds so you can pay taxes separately (and penalties, if applicable). This can be ordered in your QDRO.

Touch and Feel Time

The final, all-important point to consider is exactly when you can gain access to the money and whether you'll have to pay a penalty to do so. Ironically, if the plan belongs to your husband, depending on the specific plan provisions, it may actually be easier for you to access the money now than it is for your husband to get it if he's not yet at retirement age. Your QDRO can stipulate that you are entitled to receive your distribution as soon as your property division is finalized. You can expect to pay taxes on it, but it can be a good source of immediate cash. Your husband, on the other hand, will probably have to wait until he reaches age 59½ before he can access his share of the retirement plan funds without penalty.

If you would rather not take a lump sum distribution from a retirement plan now, you can choose to wait until your husband retires and receive your share of his pension plan proceeds at that time. This may make sense if your husband is close to retirement age and you don't need the money immediately and don't want to have to pay taxes on a lump sum distribution now.

If for whatever reason you are not interested in your husband's retirement plan—perhaps because you're not too thrilled with his investment choices—you could negotiate to have your husband keep his pension plan in exchange for other assets. These assets could be in the form of either cash or property. If you have your own pension plan, you and your husband don't need to haggle over dividing the assets of both plans equally between the two of you. Instead, you can each keep your own plan, and if his is worth more, you can negotiate for other assets to equalize the value.

Which assets should you be interested in? Certainly not the junky stuff many men try to dump on their unsuspecting wives during settlement negotiations. "Jack 'generously' offered to give me all of his stinkiest, most illiquid investments because he said they would turn around and be worth a fortune," laughed Kaitlyn, thirty-six, an assistant office manager for a Fortune 500 company. "Generous, my foot! He was trying to unload his worst losers on me while he kept the blue-chip stocks and Treasury bonds for himself. I told him, 'Good try, Jack, but no sale,' and insisted on half of the stocks and bonds instead."

Securing Your Future

Even though they will typically satisfy only a small percentage of your actual retirement needs, it's important to find out if and when you are entitled to Social Security benefits. If your husband is already receiving benefits and you were married for at least ten years, are at least sixty-two years old, and have not remarried since your divorce, you'll be eligible for benefits based on the amount and duration of your husband's Social Security contributions. You can start collecting benefits at sixty-two, but this amount will typically equal only 37.5 percent of the amount your husband is eligible to collect. If you wait until you're sixty-five, the payment will equal 50 percent of his benefits. Bear in mind, though, that if your husband is *not* yet collecting Social Security, then you cannot begin receiving benefits until you have been divorced for at least two years. And if you're already receiving your own Social Security, you will *not* be entitled to benefits under your husband's policy unless they are greater than yours. In that case, you get his but not yours. You can't double dip.

A final word on retirement plans: If retirement plan assets are to be divided between you and your husband, keep your eyes open and don't get snookered! You don't want to get stuck with investments of dubious value that are almost impossible to sell in any market—except at maybe ten cents on the dollar. Make sure that you get your fair share of the highest-quality stocks, bonds, and mutual funds in the retirement plan. Don't settle for less.

Debt and Taxes

We've done a fair amount of talking about dividing up assets like your home, your business, and your retirement plans. But what about dividing up your debts? Remember to think about who gets the car payments, not just who gets the car.

When you start to divvy up the debts, first figure out whose debts they are—yours, mine, or ours. Any debt acquired by just one of you—either before or after the marriage—is owed only by that person. But you're both liable for any debts accumulated while you were married. During separation, you're back to separate debts—whoever incurred the debt pays it. The one exception is debt incurred to pay for family necessities like food and shelter for you and your children. If you can't afford to pay these debts yourself, it's generally assigned to your husband.

This is all pretty simple, eminently logical, and largely theoretical. It sounds good on paper, but what happens when your husband agrees to pay a particular debt he took on while you were married and then he reneges? Is it his problem? No, now it's your problem. In fact, creditors will come after *you* if your husband defaults on any debt incurred while you were married. (More about this below.)

Sorting It All Out

If you're like most people, the very mention of taxes sends you into a state of near cardiac arrest. Don't panic! Even if your tax picture is a major mess and nearly impossible to understand, it will all get sorted out.

First of all, remember that you're not alone. Your accountant is an invaluable member of your "A team," so be sure to turn to her for help sooner rather than later. Do not—I repeat, *do not*—let the same accountant advise both you and your husband even if it seems like the logical and cost-effective thing to do. Remember that your husband is *not* a member of your "A team," and you do *not* have the same financial interests. Sharing one accountant is an accident waiting to happen, especially when settlement negotiations heat up.

If you file for divorce in the middle of a tax year, you can either file a joint return or choose to file separately. This should not be a decision based on emotion. It should be based on arithmetic, pure and simple. It's your accountant's job to determine what method of filing is in your best financial interest.

Some accountants advise against filing a joint return, especially in cases where the husband has a tendency to take aggressive deductions. Remember, if you file a joint return, you have joint liability, and the IRS may come after you at some future point for back taxes, penalties, *and* interest. For this reason alone, it makes sense to file taxes separately the year of your divorce.

You certainly don't want to risk finding yourself in the same boat as my client Melanie. Unbeknownst to Melanie, her husband, Dale, lied on their tax return in a blatant attempt to stiff Uncle Sam. Three years after the divorce, the IRS came after Melanie. Why Melanie and not Dale? Because by that time Dale had declared bankruptcy, leaving Melanie holding the IOU to the IRS. They promptly put a lien on both the house that she had received in the divorce settlement and on her flower delivery business. Her response? "I didn't know what was going on. All I did was sign where Dale told me to sign. Why should I be expected to pay when my husband was the one cheating the government?"

The way the IRS sees it, if you can read a tax return, you're responsible for understanding what it says. If you don't understand what the numbers mean, you're supposed to ask. That's reality. Anything beyond a Forrest Gump IQ, you're expected to know what's going on. So if you have any reason to suspect that your husband may be pulling a fast one, insist on filing separate returns—and read yours before you sign it!

If you do decide to file separately, you have the option of amending your return and filing jointly anytime within the next three years. But if you file jointly, you cannot reconsider and file a separate return later. So, again, when in doubt, file separately.

Discuss your preference with your husband, and once you've agreed on a method of filing, put it in writing.

If You Do File Jointly

If your accountant firmly believes it's in your best financial interest to file a joint return, do so with your eyes open and your antennae up. Even if you have no reason to suspect dishonesty on your husband's part, be on the alert. You'd be surprised how many squeaky clean husbands cheat on their returns.

And, again, don't think that being innocent of the facts will let you off the hook if the IRS comes after you at some future date. "I didn't know" just doesn't cut the mustard anymore. In most cases, the IRS will assume that if you can sign your name, you can read. And if you can read, then you know what's on your tax return.

Betty Weiss of Coconut Creek, Florida, who ironically was married to an IRS auditor prior to her divorce, claimed that she had no idea her husband, Meyer, was hiding bribe income from—you guessed it—the IRS. Betty also claimed that she never asked Meyer how they could afford a country club membership on his government salary and never suspected that something was rotten in the state of Florida. The U.S. Tax Court ruled that if Betty *didn't* know what was going on, she certainly *should* have; she was held equally liable for more than $150,000 of unpaid taxes and liabilities from five years of joint tax returns. She signed the returns, so she has to pay the piper.[10]

But what if you weren't the one who signed your name? Then you're protected because there *is* a forgery rule. This means if your husband forged your signature on a joint return and you had no personal income reported on that return, you are not liable for any taxes owed. (If you did have personal income, you are liable for taxes owed only on that amount.) There is also a duress rule which holds that if you signed a return under pressure or threat from your husband, and you wouldn't have signed otherwise, you're not liable for the taxes, either.

Absent a case of forgery or duress, however, you are liable

for the taxes owed on a joint return, assuming you knew that the tax return was being prepared and filed *and* assuming that you actually signed it. You're then liable for the *entire* amount of the taxes owed—not just your share but his, too.

Who Gets to Deduct What?

If you and your husband choose to file separately, you need to decide who will declare your children as dependents and who gets to take them as an exemption on their tax return. (See page 157 for more information on declaring your children as dependents.) Likewise, you must determine who will get to deduct the interest portion of the mortgage payments as well as the property taxes you paid jointly. These decisions and many others regarding how various items should be treated for tax purposes will be worked out during your settlement negotiations. This underlines again the need for having your own accountant who is 100 percent on your "A team."

What if Uncle Sam Owes You?

If you file jointly, remember that what's good for the goose is good for the gander. Just as you'd both be liable for paying joint taxes, you'll both be eligible for a tax refund if you're entitled to one. It's treated as joint property.

If you weren't expecting a tax refund and consider it a windfall, why not use the money to pay off debts or to add to your retirement savings? If you want to spend some of it on a minor splurge, go for it. But use my second D—discipline—and don't overdo it.

And on the subject of taxes: Put whatever decisions you make about how to file and who gets which deductions in

writing even if your husband says that he'll take care of everything and you trust him to the moon and beyond.

Better to be a champ than a chump.

Who Pays the Piper?

What if your husband ran up a mountain of debts while you
were married and now claims he has no money to repay
them? Are you left holding the bag? Probably.

Your specific obligation to pay your husband's debts varies
from state to state, and so does the vulnerability of your property. In some states, creditors can actually seize your separate
property to pay for your husband's debts. No kidding! Is that
unbelievable or what?

The best way to protect yourself is to be prepared. Forewarned is forearmed. If you haven't done so already, make a
list of debts that you and your husband owe jointly. Also list
your separate debts such as college loans or family loans incurred while you were still single. Write down to whom the
money is owed and how much money you still owe. Then as-
sign one or both of you to repay each debt. Again, this works
in real life only if both of you act in good faith. If you suspect
that your husband is likely to say "okay" now but "no way
I'm paying for that" later, forget about using this method unless you still believe in the tooth fairy. Instead, you'll be much
better off protecting yourself by paying all debts now, *before*
the divorce is final. This way, you won't get stuck holding the
bag later.

It's your call, but when you're deciding what to do, remember the risk you run if you agree to let your husband pay
any or all of the debts. If he doesn't pay, you're liable. Protect
yourself. Find out if there are any legal paths you can take to
make sure that your husband pays the debts he owes. But
again, the best way to ensure that you're not hassled by cred-

itors later is to make sure that all the debts are paid now. If that means doing it yourself, do it! If you're lucky, your settlement agreement will compensate you for settling these debts. If not, at least you've gotten the bad news out of the way now.

Alimony: What Is It? Who Gets It?

Up until the last twenty or so years, alimony was pretty much the norm. He gave; she got. End of story. If June Cleaver had divorced the Beaver's dad, she would have had no other source of income except alimony. True, she looked great in those shirtwaist dresses and pearls, but she apparently had no marketable skills—at least none that we ever heard about. Her job was to be a full-time wife and mother, which was socially acceptable in the 1950s but certainly didn't pay very well. For her, alimony wasn't an option—it was a necessity.

Fast forward to the 1990s. Let's see how much has changed.

While it has become almost an economic necessity for both marriage partners to bring home a paycheck in the 1990s (particularly younger couples just starting out), many fortysomething plus women have never worked outside the home and have no means of support other than their husband's income. They're in pretty much the same boat as June Cleaver when you come right down to it.

The difference is that alimony *isn't* the norm in the 1990s. With over 60 percent of all American women—and fully 75 percent of all women twenty-five to forty-four years old—employed outside the home, the expectation is that women are ready, willing, and able to support themselves.[11] And if they're not, they certainly should be. That's all well and good as a theory, and it certainly wins points for political correctness, but let's not rush too quickly to judgment.

"They rewrote the rules while I wasn't looking," says Barbara, a vivacious fifty-four-year-old with model-perfect posture and the complexion of a woman 20 years her junior. "When I think about it, I sound like the prototypical Stepford wife: two children, corporate spouse, business dinners, carpools, Halloween costumes, room mother, the whole nine yards," she says. "And today, none of that counts. He walks out on me and, bingo, I'm supposed to look for a job. Doing what? I'd like to know. Chauffeur, seamstress, professional smiler?"

Many divorcees find themselves in a situation very similar to Barbara's, yet women receive alimony in only 15 percent of all divorces today. In the state of California, for example, only one out of every six divorced women receives any form of ongoing spousal support whatsoever.

In some cases, alimony may be paid until your husband's death or your own remarriage, unless you and your husband agree to other terms. This occurs most often when a divorced woman has been in a long marriage and is deemed to have few or no marketable skills.

So-called rehabilitative alimony is paid while you go back to school or acquire job training or retraining so you can enter the workplace. You're paid the alimony only until your new job provides the income you need to live on.

Some states award alimony as a means of repaying you for putting your husband through school or making other sacrifices to further his career, perhaps even at the expense of your own. Contributions you've made to the family, including taking care of the children or keeping up the house, can also be compensated with alimony.

How Much Alimony Will You Get?

First of all, don't confuse alimony with marital property or assets. They are completely separate issues.

When you legally separate or file for divorce, the court can order that spousal support be paid. *This* is alimony—in this case, temporary alimony. The amount is based on how much you need and how much your husband can afford to pay. So if you have a job with a salary that pays your living expenses, you won't be eligible for much in the way of support.

Similarly, if you have a law degree but haven't practiced for the past few years because you wanted to take a crack at writing a novel, the court may determine that your earning potential warrants your receiving much less alimony than someone with no job training or skills.

The court will also look at the assets you and your husband are dividing in your divorce. Let's say you negotiate to keep your house in exchange for your husband's keeping the rest of your joint assets. Even if you have no job and limited earning potential, selling the house and investing the proceeds could theoretically provide enough income to live on for quite some time. In some cases, therefore, the court will take this into consideration when determining how much financial support you'll need.

There are other issues that factor in as well. The length of your marriage is a major one. Generally speaking, a marriage of ten years or longer has potential for receiving significantly more alimony—that is, alimony paid over a longer period of time—than a relatively short marriage.

There's Only So Much to Go Around

Another relevant factor is how deep your husband's pockets are and who's already reaching into them. The court will recognize that your husband can pay only so much to so many people. Maybe he's paying child support for your children. Maybe he's also supporting his elderly father by paying his nursing home costs. Or maybe he's obligated to pay college tuition for his two children from a previous marriage. All of these support payments essentially come out of the same place—your husband's pocket—so his other financial commitments will almost certainly affect the amount of alimony you can expect to receive from him.

What You Can Do

Here is where it comes in very handy to have documented your standard of living during your marriage. If you can adequately demonstrate that while you were married you became accustomed to a certain lifestyle, you have a much better chance of receiving enough alimony to maintain that lifestyle after your divorce. If you haven't assembled the paperwork already, do it now. Credit card receipts and canceled checks can be used to document travel, clothing, and average living expenses over the past several years.

Some expenses will change as you go forward; others won't. If you have been spending $500 a month on groceries for four and now you'll be buying only for three, it's likely that your anticipated food expenses will be lower. Your mortgage payment, on the other hand, will not. Based on what you think your new cost of living will be, try to create as accurate an estimate as possible of what you'll need to live on and how much you'll require in alimony.

Remember to take into account any money coming in from your job or from assets that you plan to cash in. This will give you a pretty clear estimate of what you have and what you still need. Alimony payments can fill the gap.

Small Checks or Big Assets?

Alimony comes in different shapes and sizes. There is the classic concept of alimony as a monthly payment that continues until your husband dies or until you remarry. But that's not the only way to get what's coming to you. Many women prefer to receive their alimony in a single lump sum. The benefit of doing it this way is you don't have the constant headache of worrying whether your ex-husband will "forget" to send the check again this month. And, of course, the lump sum is yours to have and to hold from this day forward regardless of whether or when you choose to remarry. Also, cutting off the purse strings goes a long way toward mending broken heart-strings. So if you have your druthers, take the money and run.

My client Cathy negotiated for a lump sum settlement until she was blue in the face. She finally gave up and agreed to monthly alimony. Three years later she is still sorry that she did. "The monthly checks are a vivid reminder that my ex-husband still holds the financial reins even though we're divorced," she says. "I have to remind myself constantly that he's paying me money that is rightfully mine, money I deserve for putting him through med school and taking care of the family for twenty years. I really hate the fact that he still doles it out just like he did while we were married."

Cathy makes a good case for accepting nothing less than a lump sum settlement. The most important point, as far as I'm concerned, is that a lump sum settlement, unlike monthly alimony, gives you complete jurisdiction over your own money—immediately and finally. You can do exactly as you please, investing or spending the money any way you wish.

Be sure, though, to check with your "A team" accountant regarding any potentially negative tax consequences associated with receiving a lump sum distribution. There's no point negotiating your guts out if Uncle Sam takes the lion's share.

If it is *not* in your best financial interest or if you are unable to negotiate a lump sum settlement, there are several things you should carefully consider before agreeing in writing to monthly alimony.

You definitely want your alimony payments to reflect the rising cost of living due to inflation. If you agree to $900 a month this year, what will that same amount buy you in fifteen years? And if your husband owns a fledgling business you helped him get off the ground, how will you feel if it starts booming eighteen months from now? Or what happens if you move in with someone but don't remarry? Will you be putting your alimony in jeopardy? Consider these and other possibil-

ities when you're negotiating for how much alimony you'll receive and how long you'll receive it.

Also, if you'll be relying on your ex-husband for monthly
alimony, it pays to protect your source of income. This is
where a QDRO can prevent a potentially serious gap in your
cash flow, assuming your ex's pension plan administrator is
willing to be cooperative. Your QDRO can stipulate in writing
that you'll be entitled to receive part of your husband's pension if he doesn't pay the alimony that he owes you. And you
can also take out an insurance policy on your husband's life,
naming yourself as beneficiary. This will guarantee you a
source of funds should he die prematurely. Again, don't think
that you're doing something ruthless or ghoulish. You're protecting yourself financially. No more, no less—and certainly
no more than you deserve.

Another Option: The Alimony Substitution Trust

A great way to receive alimony payments without having to
wait for that ubiquitous monthly "it's in the mail" check from
your husband is to use an alimony substitution trust. This is a
trust custodianed at a bank or brokerage firm. Your husband
establishes an account, typically funded with a portfolio of in-
come-producing stocks and bonds. These investments, in turn,
generate dividends and interest income sufficient to "pay" you
each month's agreed-upon alimony amount. But the trust is
paying you alimony each month, not your ex-husband, so you
don't have to rely on his good memory or worry about staying
in his good graces in order to receive your monthly check.

So far, so good. But what if the investments in the alimony
substitution trust don't generate enough income to provide
the alimony you've agreed to? The provisions of the trust will
protect you if this happens by allowing you to sell any or all of
the investments in the portfolio to raise cash as needed.

What's the catch? The investments have to be liquid. In plain English, you have to be able to sell them quickly if necessary. So make sure that your ex-husband doesn't load your alimony substitution trust with illiquid investments that are difficult to sell at the best of times and almost impossible to get rid of at the worst of times.

In my opinion, using an alimony substitution trust to generate (and safeguard) your income is a far superior option to waiting for your ex-husband to come through with a check every month. But the best option by far is the lump sum settlement, which means that you get the bucks now and the bucks stop with you.

The Taxman Cometh

One very important caveat about receiving alimony, whether you agree to take it in the form of a lump sum settlement or via monthly checks from your ex-husband or an alimony substitution trust: Alimony is taxable as income. That means when you get paid, Uncle Sam will expect to get paid, too. So when you estimate how much alimony you'll need to meet your living expenses, don't forget to factor in taxes. And don't plan on spending your entire alimony check. Keep a tax reserve in your money market account that gets left untouched until you have to pay your IOU to the U.S. government come April 15.

Protecting Your Children

No matter what went wrong in your marriage, the one sure thing you and your husband should absolutely agree on is the need to protect and provide for your children. Forget about who did what to whom, and focus on doing what's best for your kids—both emotionally *and* financially.

The two main issues relating to child support are custody and money. Who will the children live with, and who will be financially responsible for their support (and, consequently, claim them as tax deductions)? Until fairly recently, this was a no-brainer. Mom got physical custody; Dad got legal custody. Or, in plain English, Mom got the kids; Dad got the bills. But that's not always true today. Some parents have joint physical custody arrangements and agree to share legal and financial responsibility. And for some families, that works out fine.

Base these decisions on what works best for you, but also think it through from your child's perspective. Does the benefit of being able to spend equal time with both parents outweigh the confusion and hassle of shuttling back and forth between Mom and Dad?

When my client Anita described what her sister's kids go through every week, I could hardly believe my ears. "Every other day, they commute from their mom's house to their dad's house. But then my sister and her ex-husband are always switching who gets them on which days because since the divorce they both travel a lot on business and constantly need to revise their schedules. It's to the point where the kids don't know if they're coming or going. I'd love to spend time with them, but I think it would be even more confusing to throw me into the mix."

Most custody arrangements are a lot less complicated than this one, but Anita's story certainly points out the need to think seriously about what you'll be doing for—and to—your children when you agree on who gets whom, when, and for how long.

Don't Let Your Emotions Run Roughshod over Your Common Sense

When you are making provisions for your children, the most important thing you can do is set aside your feelings about your husband and your marriage and think about what's best for your kids. (Nobody said this was going to be easy.) Let go of your anger and, by all means, let go of any need you may have to be deferential to your husband. You won't be doing your children any favors by tiptoeing around him, trying not to be too demanding. It's your job to make sure that they get what they need.

It's natural to want to protect your children and to keep them as far away as possible from any controversy or unpleasantness, to say nothing of downright ugliness. But it's up to you to protect their financial interests. Remember, the man you're divorcing is still their father, and he still has the responsibility to provide for them.

This is not the time for you to be a good sport. Even if you feel guilty about your marriage not working, *don't* let your feelings convince you to settle for less than your children deserve.

Likewise, don't let your anger over the divorce or your resentment toward your husband cause you to demand unreasonable support or, worse, to deny your husband visitation rights. These antics will only antagonize your husband, and he'll be less willing—or even unwilling—to write you a check even if it's for your kids. Bottom line: Your children will be hurt, and that's clearly too high a price to pay. You can be independent. Your children cannot.

Know What You Need

You might have a general idea of how much you spend on your children, but when you sit down and actually crunch the numbers, you may be in for quite a surprise. Just because kids are younger than we are doesn't mean they cost less. *Au contraire.* And the older they get, the more expensive they get. My two teenage sons have taken to starting almost every sentence with the words "I want" or "I need." Never a cheap proposition.

When you calculate what you're likely to need in child support, begin by listing every expense you can possibly think of, starting with the fixed monthly expenses for the household, including your mortgage, insurance, food, and utilities. Then add in strictly "kid expenses" like clothing, child care, tuition, tutors, doctor and dentist visits, and even movies, Super Nintendo games, and weekly allowances. And be sure to include the extras that they're used to like summer camp, piano and karate lessons, school trips and orthodontic braces, none of which comes cheap. Neither do therapy sessions, by the way, so if your child sees (or will be seeing) a therapist regularly or is in a substance abuse treatment program, don't forget to add in these costly expenses as well.

This list will give you a clear idea of how much money you'll need to support your children. Subtract the monthly income that you know you can count on from all sources, including your job, alimony, and so forth. Then you can determine how much you'll need in child support to make up the difference.

Thinking Ahead

What are your children's talents and interests? Is she a computer wizard? Does he aspire to turn his flair for the dramatic into a screenwriting career? Try to think ahead and make financial provisions for hobbies, classes for gifted students, and extracurricular sports and enrichment activities. If you and your husband had planned to send your kids to private school next year, don't change your plans and shortchange your kids. If you can swing it financially, work it into your support agreement.

Thinking ahead also means planning ahead. Thankfully, unlike alimony, child support payments are *not* taxable, so you don't have to worry about unwelcome surprises at tax time. But you do need to be concerned about cost-of-living increases due to inflation. I can't overstress the importance of making sure that child support payments increase to keep pace at least with the rate of inflation (currently at just under 3 percent). You should negotiate to have support payments increase each year even above and beyond basic cost-of-living adjustments. Remember, with kids, the bigger they get, the more they cost.

The College Years

In most states, child support ends when your children turn eighteen; in some states, it continues until they are nineteen or graduate from high school. But realistically, as any parent can tell you, that's not where the expenses end. Not by a long shot. How many eighteen-year-olds are ready to support themselves? Especially if they want to go to college and then on to graduate school, law school, or—horror of horrors— medical school! Tuition costs keep climbing every year, typically much more than the overall inflation rate. Consider, too, all the other expenses associated with college and beyond, including textbooks, food, housing, clothing, travel, phone bills, social clubs/fraternity fees, and so on.

With this in mind, it's clearly a good idea to incorporate a written agreement into your settlement stipulating who will pay for your children's education, how it will be financed, and for how long. Unfortunately, by the time they reach college age your children are no longer legally considered dependents, so it's virtually impossible to force your husband to pay for their education if he refuses. Even if he agreed previously, you can't make him do it if he won't.

How can you protect your children and ensure their education will be provided for? An excellent method is to establish an education trust in which you, your husband, or both of you contribute to a growing fund for your children's education.

Keep in mind that if you both contribute to the trust, you will obviously have to communicate with your husband and agree on how the trust funds will be invested. If this doesn't sound too good to you or if you're worried that he won't live up to his end of the bargain, you can just as easily open two trust accounts and contribute to them separately. Whether you establish one trust account or two, it is best to fund it immediately—during or directly after the divorce. That way, your children's education is secure, and you don't have to worry about finding the money to pay for it later on. Life happens, unanticipated expenses crop up, and it gets harder and harder to put away money for the kids. Do it now and know that it's done.

Insuring Your Children's Future

What happens to your children's financial security if your husband, who has had primary responsibility for their financial well-being, suddenly dies? Good question. If the children have fully-funded education trusts, you know that their future educational costs are covered. But what about their expenses now, today, this month? They—and you—can be in a real financial bind, especially if your husband didn't create an estate plan to provide for your children in the event of his death.

How can you prevent this from happening? By literally insuring your children against losing their financial support in the event that your husband dies prematurely. You can take out an insurance policy on your husband's life that will act as an emergency fund for your children if it is needed. State law permitting, the best way to do this is for you to be both the owner and the beneficiary of the policy as custodian for your minor children until they reach twenty-one. This will help guarantee that their financial needs will be taken care of even if their father is no longer alive to take care of them.

Reality Check: Will He Pay?

Education trusts and insurance policies are both great ways to protect your children's future financial needs, but how can you make sure that this month's child support check will be there when you need it? Or next month's? Or the month after that? I wish I had an easy answer. Unlike alimony, which you have the possibility of receiving in a lump sum, child support is paid month by month, in dribs and drabs, with no guarantees.

All too often, child support is *not* paid. In the state of California, only one-third of all divorced fathers pay any child support whatsoever. The problem isn't limited to California—it's a national disgrace. In fact, the issue of calling "deadbeat dads" to task legally has finally become a line item on the national political agenda, as well it should be.

Unfortunately, as of now, there are very few legal means of ensuring that even court-ordered child support actually gets paid. President Clinton recently called on Congress to tighten enforcement of child support laws by requiring states to revoke the driver's licenses of absent parents who are delinquent in their payments. And since 1994, all child support orders nationwide contain an automatic wage withholding provision. That means child support can be automatically deducted by your husband's employer and sent directly to you each month. If your husband is unemployed but receives Social Security or payments from a pension plan or annuity, child support may be withheld by court order as well. The IRS can also lend a hand. If your ex-husband is due a tax refund, the IRS can deduct overdue child support payments before sending him his check.

Non-payment of child support is considered contempt, so do consider contacting your local district attorney's office to report your ex-husband if he isn't making his payments. You can take legal steps and follow specific procedures established by law to go after delinquent fathers. It's certainly worth a try.

I wish I could say there's good news on the horizon regarding custody and child support issues, but many family law experts fear that quite the opposite may be true. With the advent of vocal "fathers' rights" groups and the publicity generated by high-profile custody cases such as that of Simpson lead prosecutor Marcia Clark, the trend seems alarmingly toward reducing child support payments, especially to working mothers. In some cases, the courts are even being asked to award primary custody to stay-at-home men who claim their ex-wives are too busy working to care adequately for their children. This strikes me as a particularly specious argument given the fact that twenty-three million mothers work, including 80 percent of all divorced mothers.[12] The irony is that most divorced women have to work whether they choose to or not. How else are they supposed to support themselves and their children post-divorce? The bottom line is they are forced to work and then are punished for doing so.

Truly, there aren't a lot of options for women who consistently get shortchanged on child support—if they get anything at all. If there is any solution, it's trying to the best of your ability to negotiate for as large a settlement as you can possibly get at the time of your divorce. Trying to get what you and your children deserve after the fact can be a harrowing, frustrating, and ultimately fruitless experience.

My Ten Commandments for Making MoneySmart Divorce Decisions

Divorce is about making decisions. And more decisions. "It got to a point where I couldn't even decide if I was coming or going, much less who gets to keep the master bedroom furniture and who gets to keep the mutual funds," recalls Sally. "I finally needed to tell everyone around me just to leave me alone so I could think straight," she says.

As you move forward in the divorce process to the all-important final negotiations, the decisions may not get any easier, but your ability to stay focused and stay on track will. Take a deep breath. You're almost there. And remember, just because you're continually barraged by the opinions of everyone around you doesn't mean you need to follow them or even listen to them.

Unfortunately, no one can decide everything for you. But I can help. Start by following my **Ten Commandments for Making MoneySmart Divorce Decisions:**

1. **Don't get overwhelmed.** Take it one step at a time. Make today's decisions today, tomorrow's decisions tomorrow.

2. **Prioritize.** Not every decision is equally important in the overall scheme of things. Don't sweat the small stuff.

3. **Ask questions and keep asking questions.** It's the only way you'll get the answers.

4. **Don't feel obligated to follow other people's advice.** That's why they call it advice, not gospel.

5. **Trust your instincts.** When all is said and done, the buck stops with you.

6. **Decide what's financially best for you (and your children).** It's not your job to take care of your husband anymore. He'll take care of himself.

7. **Don't be put on the defensive.** If you're comfortable with your decisions, you don't need to explain yourself to anyone.

8. **Don't be shortsighted.** Think about how your decisions will affect your financial well-being—now and in the long term.

9. **Accept that not every decision you make will be the "right" decision.** If you make a mistake, try to correct it. If you can't correct it, let it be. Beating yourself up won't make it better.

10. **Look ahead, not backward.** Don't make decisions that reflect old wounds and old behavior. Letting go of the past can only make your future brighter.

PART IV

- - -

Resolution

Moving from Two to One

Your divorce is nearing its completion, but you still have one very major hurdle—negotiating your final settlement.

Settling Doesn't Mean Settling for Less

The phase of your divorce in which you actively negotiate your final settlement is when it all starts seriously coming together—or seriously falling apart. This is *not* the time to start settling for less than you want or deserve. On the contrary, you've kept things together this long, you can hang in there just a little longer. After your settlement is signed, sealed, and delivered, you can start enjoying your freedom and independence from the old and start looking forward to the new. The light at the end of the tunnel is in sight. Just a few more steps and you'll be there.

Start by assessing all the information that you and your

lawyer, accountant, appraiser, and other "A team" members have gathered. Look closely one last time at your joint property and assets, and formulate a final proposal for how you'd like to divide them. Figure out your best case, your next best case, and your "no way in hell will I accept this" scenarios. Your husband will have different ideas about what works for him. (How's that for understatement?) So you'll begin negotiating. You'll draft a proposal, he'll draft a counterproposal, and you'll negotiate until you've reached a settlement that you can both live with.

First Things First

Before you meet with your lawyer to formulate a serious settlement offer to present to your husband, you have to develop a sense of which assets you truly want, which ones you can live without, and where you are willing to make concessions. What's your bottom line? What is the absolute minimum that you're willing to accept? Here's where you need to trust your warm fuzzies and your good common sense to tell you where to stand fast and where to bend. And even if your lawyer tells you that you'd be insane to accept anything less than XYZ, do a comfort level check and figure out what you really want to do and how you really feel because, ultimately, this is your settlement and you have to live with it.

You also have to be firm in your resolve not to be bullied into accepting less than you deserve. On paper, all assets look alike. There are a hundred and one ways to swap this set of silverplated flatware for those shares of stock. And if you just take a quick look at the tally sheet and see that everything looks equal, you may feel satisfied, at least initially. But stop, go back slowly, and think about each item on the list. Think about the present and think about the future—your cash needs today and your retirement years to come. Think about sentimental but essentially worthless keepsakes and think about investment pieces that you hand-picked after weeks of careful research. You can't keep everything, but you can negotiate hard for the best settlement for you.

"Cash Is King"

At this point, you know exactly what you and your husband own, and you have a handle on all the assets that will be divided. When you put together your wish list of assets that you'd like to keep, remember that "cash is king." If I'm not mistaken, these words of wisdom were originally Donald Trump's. This was before his divorce, back in the old days when Ivana actually still called him "The Donald." (Can you believe that?) In any event, my opinion of Donald Trump as marriage material notwithstanding, the financial wisdom of his statement is certainly beyond reproach.

Receiving your settlement in cash is almost always your best case. It gives you the broadest options for building your financial future. It's the ultimate fresh start with a clean slate—definitely something to shoot for.

Remember that your divorce is a gateway to your new life. You want the most freedom you can possibly have to design that life to suit you—or the "new you" that you want to be. In financial terms, that means having the ability to invest cash assets today in ways that will serve you well tomorrow.

Be wary of alimony payments that sound like a lot today but in fact will be worth a lot less in the future. As the years go by, inflation and changing tax rates can easily eat away at what seems like a substantial amount right now. That's why—barring any adverse tax consequences—a settlement that includes lump sum alimony is much better than one in which alimony is paid over your lifetime. You can invest the lump sum today and make it start working for you immediately.

Avoid taking a significant part of your settlement in the form of assets that will depreciate over time, like cars, stereo sets, and computers. Also avoid potentially risky investments like strategic metals and second and third trust deeds that fluctuate too much in price or marketability to be banked on for your future. High-quality stocks and bonds are fine, but be on the lookout for mutual funds that impose exit fees upon sale. Just remember: Cash is best, high-quality, readily marketable investments are next best, and everything else is suspect at best.

Don't Sweat the Small Stuff

For smaller assets like furniture, household appliances, dishes, and cutlery, make a list of what you have and what you want. Most likely you've done this somewhere along the way, but if not, do it now. Your wish list may include everything from a living room sofa that you've owned for many years to something as sentimental as the unmatched china settings you've collected piece by piece from garage sales. Although it's just a wish list, some of your wishes *may* come true.

Your list will also include many items both of you will probably need now that you're going to be living two separate lives. I'm talking about things like a clock radio or a Mr. Coffee machine. These things are necessary but aren't of earth-shattering importance. Even though you may feel attached to some of these items, remind yourself that toaster ovens come in different shapes and sizes, but all they do is toast the bread. Don't sweat the small stuff.

And don't get caught up in a *War of the Roses*–like scene where the Kathleen Turner character ends up loving her antique-filled house more than life itself.

While you're thinking about what you'd like to take with you, also start thinking about what you're willing to leave behind. Here is where it's important to separate your money from your emotions. Don't insist on holding on to an easy chair that means nothing to you just because it's your husband's favorite. A little vindictiveness may feel great at the moment, but the ill will that it creates surely won't be in your best financial interest down the road. If it's not worth fighting about, why fight about it?

After you've made your wish list, be sure to discuss it with your accountant so you clearly understand the tax consequences of retaining specific items. Keeping a stock may result in a potential tax liability if you sell it later at a profit; holding on to a family heirloom that you have no intention of ever selling will cost you zero in taxes.

Taxes: The Reality Check

The tax repercussions of divorce are not always obvious or logical, but they *are* reality. Somehow that delightful little painting that hangs over your living room fireplace may seem a little less special when you're forced to sell it and then find yourself up to your Van Gogh's ears in capital gains taxes.

During your final settlement negotiations, you will certainly discuss the issues of alimony and child support. It's important to remember that alimony is taxable to you as income, while child support payments are not. If your children are dependents and they live with you, however, you may get to list them as dependents on your personal tax return, which qualifies you to take an exemption for each of them. But don't assume that this is the case because your husband may be claiming them as exemptions on his tax return as well. This may work for you and it may work for your ex, but no way does it work for the IRS. Depending on your specific custody and child support arrangements, only one of you will be able to claim the kids as exemptions—not both of you. In some cases, you can agree to claim Janie while he claims Johnny, but both of you can't claim Janie *and* Johnny.

Tax considerations also come into play when deciding whether to sell your house or keep it and continue living in it.

Remember, as I discussed in Part III, there are various taxes associated with staying in your home. You'll pay property taxes, which are deductible, as is the interest portion of your monthly mortgage payment. If and when you eventually sell your home, you may be subject to capital gains taxes. And as I mentioned earlier, depending on your age and how you choose to reinvest the proceeds, your tax liability may be zero or it may have lots of zeroes attached to the end of it (as in thousands or tens of thousands).

Life After Taxes

When you divide marital property, neither you nor your husband will owe any immediate taxes. That's the good news. The bad new is that you *will* owe taxes if and when you sell any part of that marital property after your divorce, assuming that it has appreciated in value since it was originally purchased. The bigger the gain, the bigger your tax bite.

So you want to be sure that the assets you receive in your final settlement are equal, *after taxes,* to the assets you're giving up. Even if it seems like an apples-to-apples deal, have your accountant run the numbers just to be on the safe side. You may be quite surprised to find that what seems like a fair deal on the surface is decidedly unfair when you factor in taxes.

Let's say that you and your husband jointly own a portfolio of stocks valued at $50,000. The obvious way to split the portfolio, he says, is to give you $25,000 worth of stock while he keeps $25,000 worth. Sounds fair, right? Not so fast. What if the stocks that you get are well up in value from when you originally bought them, while he (owing to the fact that he's such a good sport) takes the "losers"? If you both turn around and sell your stocks tomorrow, who's the real loser? You, because you'll be hit with capital gains tax on the stocks you sell. He, on the other hand, will come out way ahead because not only will he *not* have to pay capital gains tax when he sells, he'll actually realize a tax *loss*. Still sound fair? Not quite. But it happens all the time, and women frequently end up on the short end of the tax stick.

How can you avoid this? Unless you're advised otherwise by your attorney or accountant, just split the portfolio down the middle. Don't take X while he takes Y. You should both take 50 percent of X, 50 percent of Y, and so forth. That's the only really fair way to do it.

Offers and Counteroffers

You make an offer. He makes a counteroffer. When does it ever end? It ends when you reach some happy medium between your best- and worst-case scenarios and you can finally sleep at night. It's not black or white, right or wrong. It's a judgment call—your judgment.

Maybe, after you've hashed everything over for the gazillionth time during the settlement process, the final negotiation will be fairly easy. On the other end of the spectrum, if neither of you is willing to budge an inch, it may eventually end up in court, which is rarely in your best interest.

The main thing to keep in mind is *What's your bottom line?* Not your lawyer's, not your best friend's, not your aunt Alice's. *Your* bottom line. Don't go below it. Know what you want and don't be afraid of going after it. Remember, you're playing for keeps. Once the settlement is final, it's final. And in most cases, there's no going back.

If your settlement negotiation is unsuccessful and you think you'll be better off going to court, be realistic about the probable result. Your lawyer can advise you concerning the possible outcome. Consider whether it's likely to be better or worse than your husband's final settlement offer. Then make your decision. Know, though, that a trial can last up to two years and that at the end of the road, you may be stuck with a much worse agreement than you bargained for.

And remember that there are other options besides going to trial. If you and your husband can agree on a mediator to hear both sides and help reach a resolution that you'll both abide by, this may be a quicker and less expensive route. You can also "rent" a judge. This is essentially the same as using a mediator, but it's a retired judge who will accept an hourly fee and hear your case out of court. This, too, is cheaper and faster than a lengthy trial and is an option worth considering.

But even if it seems to take forever and even if you have to jump through emotional and legal hoops to arrive at a settlement that you can live with, it will be well worth the effort in the long run. Don't give up and don't give in until you have a moneysmart settlement that works for you.

At some point, all the negotiating, all the agreeing and disagreeing will finally end. And here is where life starts to get good—though it may not feel quite so good right away.

Moving from Two to One

In the immediate aftermath of your divorce, you may find yourself slightly shocked that your marriage is really over. For months you've been preoccupied with gathering documents, filing papers, and meeting with your attorney. Keeping busy with the divorce process can be a big distraction. Now that the dust has settled and you have some quiet time to yourself, it may hit you all over again: Your divorce has actually happened. For all intents and purposes, your marriage is over.

Diana, twenty-eight and the daughter of a longtime client of mine, reacted to her divorce like many young women her age do—at least those who can afford to. As soon as her papers were signed and she was officially "done" with the marriage, she put a down payment on a new condo, traded in her Ford Escort for a late-model Lexus, and started looking for a new job, even though she was perfectly happy with the one she had. She wanted to make changes in her life quickly and across the board. She also called nearly every person she knew to ask if they could fix her up with a blind date. She began filling every night of her social calendar with a whirlwind of activities, zooming around town fast and furiously.

This went on for nearly five weeks. During a breakfast meeting soon afterward, I asked her how she was feeling. "I haven't thought about Michael [her former husband] at all. I'm fine. Great. Super!" she said. She didn't look fine, great, or super. She looked exhausted. She hadn't given herself any time to catch up on her own life. But a few weeks later, it caught up with her.

Diana called me one afternoon, completely distraught because it had finally hit home that her marriage was over and she didn't feel up to handling it all—not the financial responsibility, not the loneliness, not even changing the Kitty Litter, which had always been Michael's job. The divorce was a big mistake, she said. She'd have been better off in a bad marriage than living alone. And what if she never met anyone else?

Diana's experience speaks volumes about the emotional roller coaster so typical of the aftermath of divorce. Sometimes going through the motions of keeping busy works, and sometimes you do feel fine, great, super—as though your divorce really has opened a door to a better life for you. Other times you sit by yourself, scared and alone, wondering what your life will be like, not excited by the possibilities but terrified of the unknowns. All of these feelings are perfectly normal and perfectly understandable. You *will* get through these times, and you *will* start taking charge of your future. Making financial decisions that directly affect your future is an important step. But figuring out what you want your future to look like has to come first.

Letting Things Sink In

Wending your way through the negotiation process can occupy your total attention until the time your settlement is
completed. You've been going and going like the Energizer
bunny. Only when you stop does it dawn on you that you're
done. This is it. Finis. All the negotiating, all the memos and
discussions with lawyers, and all the endless wear and tear
on your emotions can be incredibly distracting. And nerve
racking.

Before you meet with your post-divorce "A team" or consider making any important investment decisions, you should
definitely take some time to let everything sink in. During the
settlement process, you probably made decisions about
whether to sell your house and, if so, how to divide the proceeds. You may need to spend your first post-divorce months
getting this aspect of your life in order, including finding a
new place to live.

As you begin severing any lingering financial connections
with your husband, you will also need to tie up some critically
important loose ends like getting your taxes paid, whether
you've decided to file jointly or separately. You'll also need to
sit down with a list of your monthly expenses and a calcula-
tion of your income including your salary and alimony payments, if any. Run the numbers one more time to see whether
you'll still need additional income to support your standard of
living or whether you figured correctly earlier on and will be
just fine. If necessary, spend some serious time and effort considering how to fill in the financial blanks.

Taking Stock of What You Own

Until now, you, your husband, and both attorneys have been
treating your joint property as bargaining chips: "I'll give you

this if you'll give me that." Now that you have a final settlement, you also have your share of the joint property. It's no longer ours or his, it's yours. It's time to take stock of what you own and what you still need in concrete terms. Do you need to buy two new kitchen chairs or a new box spring for your bed? Do you have your grandmother's Wedgewood china but no refrigerator? Put together a list of the specific items that you still need and an estimate of how much it will cost to put your house in order.

Also take stock of your investment portfolio while thinking about your short- and long-term financial needs. To the best of your ability, evaluate what you own and assess whether your investments will help you reach your financial goals. If you don't understand what you own, jot down your questions and areas of confusion so you'll be prepared for your first post-divorce meeting with your "A team" investment adviser.

Your "A Team" Revisited

Your post-divorce "A team" may incorporate some of the same people who helped you through the divorce process. You may add a few players or eliminate ones you no longer need. The important thing to remember is why you picked your "A team" in the first place. These people are there to act as your advisers and to answer your questions. But most of all, their job is to help you in any way you need help, so you won't be out there all alone trying to make decision after decision by yourself.

The same rules apply now as when you first assembled your divorce "A team." There's no reason in the world to stick with an adviser whom you don't like or trust completely. Maybe the accountant you've known for the last twenty years proved to be a big disappointment to you during the divorce. Or maybe now that you're making decisions for yourself, you decide it's not such a great idea for you to do business with someone who knew your husband and who knew you when. Perhaps now is the perfect time for you to find a new accountant—one you can call your own.

You may feel the stakes are higher now that you're on your own. You don't have the buffer of your husband taking care of some or all of the financial matters or acting as the point man in dealing with your "A team." The responsibility is yours and yours alone, and now is when you really need to get everything under control.

The key to working successfully with your "A team" is understanding what each member of the team is doing for you. And, most important, you have to feel comfortable asking questions and insisting on answers in English, not banker-speak or brokerese. Prospective clients often come to me for financial planning or for explanations of investment terms because they do not understand what their stockbrokers or financial planners are talking about. My advice in these cases is to find a different investment adviser posthaste.

Before you settle on any adviser, remember your Two C's: stay within your comfort zone and listen to your common sense. Your sister-in-law, your parents, and your great-uncle Arthur may tell you that you simply *have* to use Cousin Jerry the stockbroker because he's an absolute genius and a consistent money maker. Trust your instincts. You may think it's a bad idea to mix business with family. Or maybe you're thrilled to death at the idea of doing business with Cousin Jerry, whom you've known since birth. Whatever your reasoning, stick to it if it makes sense to you.

Remember, you're the one investing your money and you're the one who needs to feel comfortable with the person helping you manage it. Comfort level involves communication. You need to know that your advisers can answer your questions clearly and understand your goals and needs. It sounds simple, I know, and it can be if you take the time to put together a top-notch "A team."

Why Do I Need A New "A Team" Now?

You may be thinking to yourself, "Wait a minute, didn't I just put together an "A team" when my divorce began? Why do I have to start over now?" My answer is, you don't. If you're happy with the advisers you have, it makes sense to stick with them. You may want to add a stockbroker or a certified financial planner if you don't already have one on your team, or perhaps an insurance agent or vocational counselor. My point is that if you want to reevaluate and possibly change any of the players on your "A team," now is a good time to make the change. But if it ain't broke, don't fix it.

Depending on your age and the complexity of your divorce settlement, you may need several different advisers. If you are twentysomething and have a very modest income, you may be able to limit your "A team" to an accountant and a therapist; you may not need to seek an investment adviser just yet. Then again, if your divorce settlement left you with a portfolio of stocks, bonds, and mutual funds, you will want a stockbroker or certified financial planner to review your holdings and help you determine if these investments are appropriate for you.

If you are fortysomething or sixtysomething, chances are that you have very specific investment decisions to make, involving retirement planning as well as tax and estate planning. A trusted investment adviser is clearly a must for your "A team."

You may also want to go back to school, change jobs, or reenter the workplace after protracted time out for child-rearing. A career counselor or vocational specialist can help you here. And if it's appropriate to continue seeing a therapist, do so. Don't shortchange yourself by scrimping on the emotional support that you need to manage the transition successfully from being married to being single. Bottom line, putting together your "A team" is about taking care of yourself.

Who Are the New Players?

A good rule of thumb is for your post-divorce "A team" to be there to give you financial and emotional support when you need it most, tapering off in some areas as you begin feeling more self-sufficient, and continuing on in other areas for your lifetime. Again, as you assess your individual needs, you'll want to take into account your age, the complexity of your financial situation, your career plans, and your state of emotional well-being.

Of the following "A team" possibilities, you probably already have the first three in place because they served as part of your divorce "A team." The next three may be more appropriate now that your settlement is finalized and you're ready to move on to the next phase of your life.

- **Therapist.**
- **Certified Public Accountant or tax preparer.**
- **Attorney.** I am not talking about your divorce attorney, although you may still need to consult him periodically regarding issues related to your divorce. But you will also need to consult attorneys with completely different areas of expertise. Your divorce lawyer should be able to refer you to colleagues specializing in taxation, estate planning, or other areas as the need arises.
- **Career counselor or vocational specialist.** If you are planning to change jobs, go back to school, enter the workplace for the first time or reenter after a lengthy hiatus, it makes sense to talk to someone who is an expert in the field. If you have already enrolled in school, consider using campus resources. Often you'll find a job network of recent graduates who are able to point you toward jobs in your particular field of interest.

You can also use professional employment services. But don't hesitate to ask friends and relatives for introductions or job references. From time immemorial business had always been done through some version of the old boys' network. Happily, in recent years, women have started forming an old girls' network. (There ought to be a better name!) Use it, and don't be shy about it. You're asking for a hand, not a handout.

• **Insurance agent.** An insurance agent will decipher different insurance options and can take you through the process of obtaining new coverage or evaluating existing coverage. Be sure that you have adequate health, disability, and life insurance, as well as auto and homeowner's or renter's policies.

• **Investment adviser.** There are several different types of investment professionals, with some degree of overlap in their areas of expertise:

Certified Financial Planner. A CFP must pass certificate examinations in six major subject areas in order to become licensed. These include the financial planning process, risk management, investments, tax planning, retirement and employee benefits, and estate planning. After your settlement is finalized, a CFP can help you structure a household or business budget, plan for your retirement, or formulate an investment strategy to save for your children's college tuition. Fee-only certified financial planners charge by the hour or a flat fee for a comprehensive financial plan. Fee-based or fee-plus-commission planners also charge a commission on investments (typically mutual funds and annuities) purchased through them.

Stockbroker. Most people think of stockbrokers buying and selling stocks and bonds. Traditionally, that is what they do. But they can also help you with other financial instruments ranging from gold coins to Treasury bills. You'll want a stockbroker on your "A team" if you received stocks, bonds, mutual funds, or other securities in your property settlement or if you're interested in these investments now. Most brokers are paid on a commission basis. Those who work extensively with money managers (see below) typically receive a fixed percentage of your portfolio's value in lieu of commissions.

There can be some overlap between certified financial planners and stockbrokers. Some CFPs are licensed brokers and typically manage their clients' assets using mutual funds and annuities. Some stockbrokers are also certified financial planners, offering brokerage services in addition to traditional financial planning. Consider the differences carefully when choosing your investment "A team" member. In most cases, you would do well to consult a fee-only planner for budgeting advice and comprehensive financial planning. Work with a stockbroker to implement your specific investment, savings, and retirement plans. In a nutshell, use the planner for planning, the stockbroker for investing.

Registered investment adviser (money manager). If you don't have the time or inclination to work closely with a stockbroker in selecting specific stocks, bonds, or mutual funds, consider asking your broker for an introduction to a registered investment adviser. Commonly called a money manager, a registered investment adviser might be a particularly good choice for you if you received a lump sum settlement as part of your divorce or if you kept the family home and plan to sell it shortly. Registered investment advisers essentially make all buy and sell decisions for you and generally deal with clients who invest a minimum of $2 million, $5 million, or more. In recent years, however, some money managers have accepted accounts as small as $100,000 if these accounts are established or introduced through a major brokerage firm. The fee that you are charged is a percentage of the assets that are being managed for you. You will also pay commission on all buy and sell transactions unless commissions are already included under a "wrap fee" arrangement.

You may choose to work with one money manager or several, depending on your specific needs and the size of your investment portfolio. Keep in mind that different managers have different investment styles. Some specialize in global investing; others buy strictly American. Some manage only stock portfolios; others invest only in tax-free municipal bonds. So choose wisely and choose appropriately.

Budgeting for Your Future by Paying Your Bills Today

During the divorce process, you made many lists. They will serve you well now. You may have been focused primarily on getting a decent settlement when you first calculated your monthly and yearly expenses, but this information will come in handy now as you figure out a budget for your daily life. Indeed, your next order of business is establishing a budget and getting used to living within its constraints.

You should already have some idea of how much money is going out to pay bills for you and your children. If you still feel a little hazy in this area, sit down again with your checkbook ledger and your credit card statements from the past several months and look carefully at every expense. This is a good time to reevaluate your spending habits. How much money are you spending on necessities and how much on purchases that you could reasonably live without? This will give you a clear picture of what you truly need to live on and what you could be saving.

I can't stress enough how important it is to pay all your bills in full each month, especially when you're first trying your new budget on for size. If you carry an outstanding balance on your credit card from month one, you'll have a hard time tracking whether your earnings and alimony are keeping pace with your spending or if you're destined to be playing catch-up forever. Until you get used to the ebb and flow of money in your checking account, you shouldn't take on any new debt. And you should try to pay off any existing debt to the best of your ability. If you can't, you can't, and that's okay. But please make a concerted effort to do so.

It always helps to have everything written down on paper, all in one place. Compare your checking account deposit slips with your credit card and bank statements every month for the first year of your new budget. That way you can clearly see how much money is going out each month, as compared to how much money is coming in. This will be a big help in establishing specific budgeting goals for yourself—for example, how much you want to save and how much you need to cut back on spending in order to meet your savings goal. There are also some fairly simple computer programs that can monitor your cash flow by keeping track of the money that goes in and out of your checking account. This only works, of course, as long as you enter the information properly. Computer programs are handy when it comes time to calculate your income taxes, too. Sad to say, though, many of us are still pretty computer illiterate, yours truly included. When I can humble myself enough to ask my fifteen-year-old son for help, I do fine; other times, I run the numbers by hand with a little help from my trusty calculator.

Sticking to a budget will help you later on if you decide to apply for a home or business loan or some other type of credit. Demonstrating to lenders that you can adhere to a serious budget will help convince them that you have your finances under control, making you a better credit risk. And you'll know you have the discipline to control your spending, so taking on new debt (if—and only if—it makes good financial sense to do so) won't seem so intimidating.

The same discipline comes in handy when you're resisting the urge to spend $100 on a new pair of really terrific boots, resigning yourself instead to putting that same chunk of money into your savings account. I know, the boots are a lot more exciting than some extra zeroes in your passbook, but they won't be nearly as important to you in the long run.

Your Savings Plan

Face it: Saving money isn't nearly as much fun as spending money. But saving money to the best of your ability today can make a big difference in the quality of your life later. Don't make the mistake of saying, "I'll save whatever's left after I pay the bills every month." Yeah, right. Saving means making a commitment to set aside a certain amount of money every month *before* you pay the bills, not after. In my house, you know how much is usually left after I pay the bills? Nada. Goose egg. Zippity-doodah. Is it any different over at your place?

I've learned to think of myself as my most important creditor, so I always pay my savings account *first* every month, not last. I figure that my future is at least as important as paying Southern California Edison. Obviously, you don't want to risk sitting in the dark as a tradeoff for contributing to your savings plan, so use your common sense. But try to stretch your savings comfort level.

The Value of a Dollar

Establishing a budget and devising a savings plan seem pretty doable. But the jump from balancing your checkbook to creating an investment portfolio is a much greater leap of faith for many women. It doesn't have to be. Using your Two C's and Two D's—common sense, comfort level, diversification, and discipline—will keep you on track as you learn investment basics and decide which financial instruments will help you meet your particular financial goals.

Begin at the beginning. Look at what you received in your settlement and decide what this money needs to do for you, now and in the future. Whether you received a lump sum settlement or are going to be receiving monthly alimony payments, you have these funds available for living expenses and perhaps for investments. Now you need to make the most of them.

Most women consistently err on the side of caution, keeping their dollars ultra-safe at the cost of allowing their dollars to grow. One of the basics of managing your investments is understanding how the value of your money can go up and down at the same time. This is not voodoo economics. It's a simple fact that if your investments aren't keeping pace with inflation, they can be going down in actual value even while their value on paper is increasing. So you can grow very poor by staying very safe.

When the Prices Go Up, Up, Up

The term inflation gets bandied about so liberally and so often that it's sometimes hard to fathom what it means to you personally. Well, I can tell you exactly what inflation means to me, to the penny. When I was eleven years old growing up in Cleveland, Ohio, a child's ticket to see *101 Dalmatians* cost 50 cents. Last week I took my eleven-year-old son to see *Mighty Ducks II*. The cost of his ticket was $3.75. We won't even talk about the price of popcorn. That's inflation! And I think it's pretty safe to assume that twenty years down the road it'll cost me a lot more than $3.75 to take my grandchild to see *Mighty Ducks XXV*.

Inflation is always expressed as a percentage. If inflation is running at 4 percent, that means the same dollar will be worth four cents less next year than it's worth this year. It also means that if your dollars are in a savings account earning less after taxes than the inflation rate, you'll have less real money—and less buying power—next year than you have now.

At only 4 percent inflation, you will need $219 twenty years from now to equal the buying power of $100 today. If inflation jumps to 7 percent, $100 worth of groceries in 1995 dollars will cost you a whopping $387 in the year 2015. When you apply this to a lump sum divorce settlement, the result can be the difference between investing wisely and allowing your money to grow, and investing too cautiously and gradually losing the lion's share of your settlement to inflation. Don't make this mistake. Make sure the value of your money is going up and only up!

Understanding Your Real Rate of Return

You can look at all the numbers in the world, from interest rates to mutual fund performance figures, but the only way to figure out what your money is doing for you is to look at its real rate of return. This is the one number that counts because it tells you what you're left with after taxes and inflation.

If you are earning 5 percent on your CD investment, you aren't going to be keeping all of that 5 percent in your pocket. If the CD isn't in a tax-deferred retirement plan, you'll have to pay Uncle Sam his share—and his share seems to get bigger and bigger. After taxes, your 5 percent return is likely to shrink to 3 percent or less. And it doesn't stop there.

You still need to subtract for inflation (currently about 3 percent) to get your real rate of return, which in this case turns out to be *less than zero*. So while you started out at a nice, steady 5 percent pace, you end up virtually right back where you started—if not even further back than that.

Understanding your real rate of return allows you to look at current and future investments with a definite eye on your bottom line. It's a commonsense approach that always works. Be prepared to reevaluate your investments from time to time as inflation rates change or as you move into a different tax bracket.

If you're one of the thousands of women who received your degree from the "don't ask, don't tell" school of marital finances, you may feel as though you're starting from scratch. Even if you were completely uninvolved in even the most basic family finances, that's okay. Your journey onward and upward through the divorce process will teach you how to take control of your own financial life and how to deal with issues that you never dealt with before.

Millions and Millions of Choices

People always use the analogy of a kid in a candy store to describe someone thrilled at the prospect of endless sweet-smelling choices. Having a lot of choices is not always a joyous thing, however. Sometimes it can be downright confusing—and intimidating. There you are in the candy store amid jars of colorful jaw breakers, ropes of red and black licorice, canisters of caramels, and vats of chocolate fudge. Think about the dilemma a child would face. Even with only seventy-five cents to spend, there must be more than ten different combinations of candy that can be bought. Instead of looking bright, sweet, and appealing, the multicolored candy jars would start to make your head spin—not to mention making you sick to your stomach.

Many women feel even more overwhelmed when confronted by what seem like millions and millions of investment choices. And that's before the world and her cousin start in with *their* surefire advice. Then look out!

You can easily sort through all these investments by knowing exactly what your choices are, what your financial needs are, and where the twain meet. If you know that you don't want something sticky to eat, you can avoid the caramel and head for the hard candy, can't you? You can use the same logic when it comes to investing.

Seeing the Trees for the Forest

No matter whether your divorce settlement consists of a lump sum of cash, monthly alimony payments, or a portfolio of stocks, bonds, and other investments, you need to understand fully your investment objectives and choices. Scary as it may be, it's certainly better to take an active role in deciding how your money will work for you than to ignore it, cross your fingers, and hope for the best.

First of all, decide what you want your money to do for you. Basically, your money can be invested to meet three different financial objectives: growth, safety, or income. Are these objectives mutually exclusive? To some extent, yes. If, for example, making your money grow is most important to you, you're going to have to take at least some risk to make it grow. And you're going to have to sacrifice some safety as well. Conversely, if your primary need right now is income, you'll have to forgo growth investments in favor of those that provide dividends and interest income. Unfortunately, you can't have it both ways. Growth investments won't keep you safe or provide much in the way of income. Investments that keep your money safe generally won't grow much, if at all. Those that provide income may also provide safety, but rarely growth. What's most important to you?

Toni, twenty-six, a claims adjuster for a regional insurance firm had been planning to apply to graduate school two years ago but opted instead to work full time while her husband, Dennis, completed law school. She and Dennis were divorced six months ago, and, happily, he agreed to help pay for her MBA program as part of their settlement agreement. The monthly checks are small—only about $750—but invested in a super-safe money market account earning 5.6 percent, the interest income will pay for Toni's textbooks. And the principal, combined with a student loan, a loan from her parents, and her own earnings from a part-time job, will pay for Toni's tuition at UCLA business school next fall.

Fixed Income Investments

If you've run the numbers six ways to Wednesday and you're still coming up short in the income department, there's no way around it. You'll have to think about investing for income, even at the expense of building a growth portfolio or a retirement nest egg. Like Toni, if you need immediate access to principal and money to live on right now, that clearly has to be your number one investment priority.

With most fixed income investments (including CDs and bonds, which will be discussed in further detail below), you will get a percentage return back (6 percent, seven percent, and so forth) in the form of interest income every six months or every year until the investment reaches maturity.

Generally speaking, if you choose top-quality fixed income investments, you will receive your entire principal back at maturity, plus a final interest payment. Beware, though: If you sell a bond or CD *before* maturity, you may get back less than you originally paid for it, especially if interest rates have gone up in the interim. So if safety as well as income is a consideration, plan on holding your fixed income investments until maturity in order to avoid losing money by selling early.

Remember that fixed income investments held to maturity pay interest, but they don't grow. Let's say that you choose to invest in a five-year Treasury note paying 7 percent interest. Maybe you choose to invest $10,000 of principal. At the end of five years, you will receive your entire $10,000 back; in addition, you will have received 7 percent interest on the $10,000 every year for those five years. Not a bad deal in terms of safety and income, but not a very good deal in terms of growth. At the end of five years, your $10,000 of principal is still $10,000. And since it's a fair bet that prices have gone up in the last five years, your $10,000 will buy less than it would have five years ago. So while income is the good news for a fixed income investment, no growth is the bad news.

Growth Investments

Growth investments do not offer a fixed rate of return, as opposed to fixed income investments that, by definition, do. As such, growth investments can loosely be termed "variable rate" investments because the rate of return isn't certain by any stretch. It changes all the time. Stocks, for example, may be considered "variable" investments or, more properly, *growth* investments. (More on stocks below.) They can—and do—go up and down in value, effectively giving you a different "return" in the form of gain or loss depending on when you sell. So while you can make more money on growth investments than on fixed income investments, you also risk losing money. Common sense dictates that you need to believe your chances of making money are greater than your chances of losing money. Otherwise, growth investments don't make sense for you.

"Safe" Investments

I've deliberately put the word "safe" in quotation marks for two very important reasons: inflation and taxes. As I mentioned earlier, perception doesn't always equal reality when it comes to a discussion of safe investments. Is it safe to lose your divorce settlement to inflation and taxes for fear of losing it in stocks and bonds? I don't think so. While you may or may not lose money by investing for growth and, to a lesser extent, by investing for income, you will certainly lose money to inflation by keeping it super "safe." So please use your common sense and, if possible, try to stretch your comfort level a little here.

When Safe Makes Sense

Now that I've made the case for not staying safe at the risk of growing poor, let me say that there should be a place in your portfolio for safe, "sleep at night" money. (I call it that because you put your head down on the pillow at night and pick it up in the morning, and your money's still nice and safe—not under the mattress but not too far away!) Regardless of whether you received your settlement primarily in cash, in monthly alimony payments, or otherwise, you'll want to keep some funds readily available for emergency money. This doesn't mean stuffing a shoebox full of five-dollar bills under your bed. It does mean exploring ways to invest your money for safety while still keeping it completely *liquid,* meaning that you can touch and feel it whenever you need it. Both banks and brokerage firms offer cash equivalents, such as interest-bearing checking accounts, short-term CDs, money market accounts, and Treasury bills.

With checking and money market accounts, you have no time constraint on when you can access your money. It's always available to you when you need it. For this reason it makes sense to keep at least a small percentage of your total assets in cash equivalents that offer daily liquidity to meet emergency expenses.

Treasury bills and short-term CDs have maturity dates ranging from one month to one year. Depending on the time frame of your investment, you'll earn different amounts of interest, with longer maturities typically paying more interest than shorter ones. Treasury bills and short-term CDs are considered cash equivalents because of their relatively short maturities, but they only offer complete preservation of principal if held to maturity. Is your money "locked up" until maturity if you choose to invest in a one-year T-bill or CD? No. You can sell it at any time before maturity, but you may have to sell it for less than you originally paid. Therein lies your risk to principal.

When Stocks Make Sense

Stocks make sense only if you have a screw loose or if you received one of the ten largest divorce settlements in the history of the human race, right? Wrong. As in the case of "safe" investments, with stocks, perception doesn't always equal reality. There are many types of stocks, some with higher risk and some with higher dividends. Stocks should definitely have a place in your portfolio if you're interested in growth. This isn't brain surgery, it's common sense. Stocks typically outpace almost all other investments and certainly have performed better over the long term than CDs, Treasury bills, and bonds. According to Ibbotson Associates, between December 31, 1925, and December 31, 1993, stocks returned an annual average of 10.33 percent versus 5.02 percent for twenty-year U.S. Treasury bonds and 3.69 percent for U.S. Treasury bills. That makes a strong case for stock investing, doesn't it?

You might be thinking, "Well, of course I want my money to grow, so why not invest all of it in stocks?" The caveat here is that where there's potential for growth, there's also potential for risk. I tend to belabor this point ad nauseam with my clients because most people focus more on the upside than the downside. You have to have a strong stomach to own stocks and a good time frame. In my opinion, you should plan on holding good commonsense stocks for a minimum of three years. You should also prepare to experience a lot of ups and downs along the way. The good news is that stocks go up a lot more often than they go down. During the sixty-eight years ending in 1993, the stock market went up in forty-eight years and down in only twenty years.[13] Those are pretty good odds, but if the roller coaster scares you, you might just want to stick to the Ferris wheel!

As a stockholder, you are either a common-stock owner or a preferred-stock owner. In either case, you own shares of a company. If the company does well, you do well. What's the difference between a common stock and a preferred stock?

Common stocks have more potential for growth but generally offer very little in the way of income. They have greater upside potential in terms of return on your investment, but they also carry more risk.

If you are a preferred stockholder, you'll receive higher dividends and experience less volatility than you would as a common stockholder. Your upside is generally limited, but you'll receive income in the form of quarterly dividends. So if you want to own stocks primarily as a means of increasing your income, you'll want to look at preferred stocks. For growth, stick to common stocks.

Common stocks come in all shapes and sizes, from "blue chip" stocks of large, household-name companies to global stocks, small company stocks, and highly speculative "penny stocks," which in my opinion should be avoided like the plague. All stocks have one trait in common: They can be winners or they can be losers. And in a down market, regardless of which stocks you own, there will be nowhere to run and nowhere to hide. Remember, stocks are great investments but not for the faint of heart.

What About Bonds?

I referred to bonds earlier when I talked about investing for income. Bonds are commonly referred to as fixed income investments because they typically have a fixed rate of return and generate a fixed amount of income. Bonds bought and held to maturity have no growth potential or inflation protection—unlike stocks, which have both. But bonds are generally less risky than stocks. And they are a good source of steady income.

When you buy a bond, it has a stated interest rate or coupon rate. So if you buy a bond with a 5 percent coupon, you will receive 5 percent interest per year, paid semiannually.

No matter what happens to inflation or interest rates while you hold your bond—whether they go up, down, or sideways—you will get your 5 percent, no more, no less.

What Exactly Is a Bond?

When you buy a bond, you are lending money to the U.S. government, to a corporation, or to a municipality for a specific period of time, ranging from less than one year to over thirty years. Bonds, like stocks, also come in many shapes and sizes, from low-risk U.S. government bonds to tax-free municipal bonds to highly speculative junk bonds.

A bond has three components: the par value, or face value, which is usually $1,000 per bond; a coupon rate, which is the interest you receive twice a year until maturity; and a maturity date, which is when you receive par value for your bond. Good income, good safety features. So far, so good.

But what if you don't need current income? Are bonds out of the picture? Not necessarily. You might want to consider *zero coupon bonds,* which pay no current interest. How do you make money on zeroes? By buying them below par value (for anywhere from twenty cents to ninety cents on the dollar) and holding on to them until maturity. They can be U.S. government bonds or tax-free municipals and are available in maturities of under one year to over thirty years.

Beware, though, of the tax consequences of owning zero coupon bonds. Although they don't pay current income, they are taxed as if they do. Your best bet is to buy U.S. government zeroes in your retirement portfolio to avoid taxation. Or you can buy *tax-free* zeroes outside your retirement plan.

Depending on your specific financial goals, it might make very good sense to buy zero coupon bonds to mature when your children will enter college. They are also a good way to plan for your own retirement. Your broker or certified financial planner can calculate exactly what they will be worth at maturity, which should be worth a lot to you in terms of peace of mind.

When the Feeling's Mutual

Lately, it seems as though mutual funds have become the investment of choice for many women. Part of the appeal is their accessibility to the beginning investor and the smaller investor. You may not have enough money to buy a well-diversified portfolio of stocks and bonds, and spending your money on just a few issues is risky. Does that mean you have to give up on investing altogether? Not at all. You may be an excellent candidate for mutual fund investing.

A mutual fund is an investment portfolio composed of many investors' dollars pooled together. Mutual funds can own stocks, bonds, international investments, or any combination thereof. They can be especially appropriate for the small investor because they require very low investment minimums—as little as $250 in some cases. In return, mutual funds offer investors the opportunity to own shares in a diversified portfolio of stocks or bonds. If you are interested in income, you'll choose a bond fund. For growth, you'll look at stock funds. If you'd like to own stocks and bonds and can afford to buy only one mutual fund, consider a balanced fund that holds a combination of both.

Remember that when you invest in mutual funds, you're leaving the day-to-day management of your investments in the hands of the fund manager. You won't be making decisions about what to buy and what to sell, and when to buy and when to sell. This is good news if you don't have the time or inclination to monitor your investments closely. It's bad news if the fund manager makes decisions that consistently end up losing you money. So even though many banks and brokerage firms offer similar-sounding mutual funds, it makes sense to look at several different funds and consider carefully before you invest.

If you do choose to invest in mutual funds, remember the first D: diversification. Don't put all your money into one fund. Look at the total amount of money that you have available to invest in mutual funds and, if possible, divide your dollars among two or more funds. You don't want the future of your investments to depend on only one fund manager. And the more diversified your investments, the less overall risk exposure you'll have in your portfolio.

Here a Fund, There a Fund

At last count, there were 2.4 gazillion mutual funds from which to select, and that number seems to be growing every day. Here a fund, there a fund . . . When you're looking at mutual funds, you'll be choosing from among several types: money market funds, stock funds, bond funds, global and international funds, balanced funds, and socially responsible funds. Your particular financial goals will be the deciding factor in determining which funds make the most sense for you.

If you want a short-term, safe, sleep-at-night investment, look at a money market mutual fund. Consider this type of fund a cash equivalent because it will allow you to protect your principal, earn interest on your money, and have check writing privileges as well. You can "park" cash in a money market fund while you are considering an investment opportunity, or you can use it as your everyday checking account. You can establish money market accounts through banks, brokerages, and mutual fund companies. If you're an upper-bracket taxpayer, be sure to ask about a tax-free money market fund.

As a rule you'll look at stock mutual funds for growth, bond mutual funds for income, and balanced funds for a combination of the two. But don't forget about global funds as a means of further diversifying your portfolio. Many excellent investment opportunities exist outside the United States, and with the globalization of the world economy, investing abroad makes good sense. As Walt Disney said many years ago, "It's a small world after all."

If you want to invest in socially responsible companies, consider doing so by selecting socially responsible mutual funds. These funds contain only stocks and bonds that have been specially screened and can include everything from "environmentally-friendly" bonds, for example, to "family-friendly" stocks of companies that provide on-premises daycare. If your warm fuzzies tell you that socially responsible mutual funds are best for you, listen up!

What You Need Is What You Get

At this point, you probably have a basic understanding of the difference between cash equivalents, stocks, and bonds. But you may very well be confused about which investments are appropriate for you. Don't be. Keep it simple. Think about your specific financial needs, your concerns, your priorities, and, yes, even your fears and anxieties about money— whether they strike you as perfectly rational or completely irrational.

Use your common sense. Figure out what's most important to you. Safety, growth, or income? If you can't have it all— and, believe me, you can't—choose what you *must* have rather than what you'd *like* to have. Use the same approach that you took in reaching your divorce settlement. Think carefully, respect your feelings, and trust your instincts. In the income-versus-growth debate, you have to go back to your financial goals. Is investing for the future your highest priority right now, or is it a distant second to your current need for income? If your monthly paycheck or alimony payment covers most of your expenses, you may not have a great need for additional income and can therefore afford to invest primarily for growth. If your alimony payments will stop in two years and you're worried about how you'll make ends meet, your number one priority may be safety followed closely by income. You probably will be unwilling to put any of your money at risk in growth investments, and who could blame you?

Jessica, sixty-two, was a former full-time Dallas, Texas, wife and mother until her husband, Frank, divorced her two years ago. She can well afford to take some risk with a portion of the hefty lump sum settlement she received. Apparently, Frank experienced a burst of generosity during divorce negotiations, no doubt owing to the fact that he ditched a forty-two-year marriage for a woman half his age and of, shall we say, uncertain reputation. Frank was, in Jessica's words, "born again, in hog heaven, and givin' away money." With more than enough income to live on for the rest of her life, generated by a substantial bond portfolio, Jessica is willing and able to invest 20 percent of her settlement in growth stocks, one-fourth of which is invested outside of the United States via a money manager and two mutual funds.

Depending on your age, your financial needs, and the terms of your settlement, you'll have different views when it comes to preserving your principal versus investing for growth or income. Whatever your needs are, there is an investment strategy that can work for you. By defining your objectives, you're taking a giant step toward achieving them.

Making Your Settlement Work for You

The key to being moneysmart during the post-divorce period is taking what you have and making it work for you now and later on. Start by relying on the Two C's and Two D's and looking to your "A team" for help in prioritizing your needs and selecting among cash equivalents, stocks, and bonds.

A well-diversified portfolio should include all three types of investments, but if that doesn't work for you right now, don't worry about it. Things change. The decisions that you make today aren't etched in stone. Nothing is forever. You can—and should—revisit your investment strategy at least once a year. If you can't invest for growth right now, maybe you'll be able to later. Don't stress about it. Do the best you can and let it be.

Ask yourself the following questions and use your answers to turn your moneysmart settlement into your moneysmart investment plan:

What are your goals in the short term? Do you have enough money to live on? Can you count on child support? Is it enough? Did you get the house as part of your settlement and need additional income to make the mortgage payments? Do you have to worry about your children's college tuition? If so, how soon? In two years or ten years? Do you have a retirement plan? How much is in it? Is it growing?

What investments did you receive as part of your divorce settlement? Do you have a stock portfolio, or did you receive a lump sum of cash that has to be invested? Do you own real estate? Can you sell it if you have to? Are your assets liquid, mostly in cash equivalents or marketable securities, or are they tied up in long-term investments that you'd rather not sell, like collectibles or artwork? How do you feel about these investments? Do they make sense? Are you comfortable owning them?

How much risk can you afford to take to achieve your short-term and long-term financial goals? Do you depend on steady income from your settlement to meet monthly expenses, or can you afford to invest at least a portion of your settlement for growth? Can you handle the ups and downs of stock ownership, or will losing money make you lose your lunch?

What are your time constraints? When will you need to touch and feel your money? In six months? In five years? When are you planning to retire? Can you afford to leave your growth investments alone for at least three to five years, or is it likely that you'll need your money sooner? What are your financial prospects? Will there be more money coming in down the road? Do you have plans to sell your house immediately, or will you wait and take the onetime tax exemption when you reach age fifty-five? Do you have any expectations of receiving an inheritance? How will your financial picture change in the years to come?

Are you sure that you're staying within your comfort zone? Have you decided what's most important to you right now: safety, income, or growth? Do you see this changing? Are you able to plan now for the future, or are your hands too full today to worry about tomorrow?

As you answer these questions, bear in mind that you're listening to today's warm fuzzies. Tomorrow's may be entirely different. I'm not advocating the Scarlett O'Hara approach to money management ("I'll think about it tomorrow"), but I am telling you to go slowly and to take some time to figure out where you're going.

Working It Out

Life after divorce—moving from two to one—brings with it changes across the board: emotional, financial, social, and, very often, vocational.

Family Business

If you and your husband owned a business or ran a professional practice together, it's likely that at least one of you has been uprooted. Statistically, that person is likely to be you.

Depending on how you agreed to handle your shared business—whether you sold it and split the proceeds, bought your husband out, or let him buy you out—chances are that things look very different now than they did before.

Even if you handled most of the day-to-day decisions of your business before, if you're now the sole owner, it's a whole new ballgame. And if you want to, you can play by a whole new set of rules. Remember to stick close to the Two C's, though. Stay within your comfort zone and use your common sense. Don't be afraid to hire a consultant or take on a new partner if it's in your own best interest to do so—and, obviously, in the best interest of your business. But if you're uncomfortable with the idea, don't do it. Listen to the advice of others but trust your instincts first and foremost.

If you sold your business or agreed to let your husband buy out your interest, remember that you can apply the same skills and knowledge that you used before to start a new business now. As long as you don't violate a non-compete clause, don't worry about stepping on your ex-husband's toes or on anyone else's. You're entitled to make a living, and you're entitled to be a success.

Time for a Change?

If you're working in a job other than the family business, this may also be a good time to reevaluate, to consider where your career is leading you. Are you happy with your job? Is your work fulfilling? Financially rewarding? Or do you absolutely loathe the idea of going to work every day but have no choice because you flat out need the money? Maybe now you should start thinking about making a change for the better.

Whether you're changing jobs or staying right where you are, you may be finding it hard to keep your mind on business when you have so many other things occupying your thoughts. Your employer, employees, and coworkers will be sympathetic, at least for a while—but only for a while. After that (maybe two weeks, two months, but not much longer), they'll expect you to suit up, show up, and get on with it. This may seem callous and needlessly insensitive, but business is business, and in the workplace, the bottom line is the bottom line. While this attitude has changed somewhat in recent years, don't be surprised if corporate compassion is short-lived.

Do the best you can. Try to leave your personal problems at home. This will not only help you take care of business, it will also occupy your mind with something other than your divorce. At the risk of sounding simplistic, I find that when I'm busy, I don't have time to worry.

Doing for Yourself

Your workplace can be a source of security and positive reinforcement for many reasons. Besides being a safe haven, a place where you can immerse yourself in something other than your divorce, it can also give you a tremendous sense of financial independence. As I mentioned earlier, your job can be the source of your health and disability insurance as well. And it can provide a means of planning for your future through pension plans and other retirement benefits.

From Bread Baker to Breadwinner

But what if you've never worked outside the home before? What if, like the little red hen, your job has always been to stay at home and bake the bread? If you're thinking about entering the workplace for the first time after your divorce, you may find yourself making the transition from bread baker to breadwinner at the same time you're making the transition from married woman to single.

If you kept the family home as the lion's share of your settlement and you don't want to sell it and live on the proceeds, you may need a job to cover your living expenses. Or your living expenses may be amply covered by your settlement, but you're feeling lost walking around an empty house all day every day. A job can go a long way toward repairing the self-esteem that got bruised through the emotional rigors of the divorce process. And having a place to go every day and knowing that you earn your own paycheck can give you a tremendous sense of independence and self-worth.

This is no small claim. Clients often tell me that after the divorce they feel completely at sea, adrift without a rudder. Those who work outside the home say that the continuity and familiarity of the workplace help get them through this transitional time.

Is now the right time to start looking for a job? If you need the money, absolutely. And even if you don't, consider the possibility. Earning money, bringing home a paycheck, is a major-league self-esteem booster. It isn't a cure-all, but it is a powerful elixir. Knowing that you can do for yourself, that you can make your own way in the world, feels pretty great especially if you've spent most of your married life believing otherwise.

"I was the perfect wife. No, I was better than perfect. I was the *ultimate* wife!" says Shana, fifty-four, a petite blonde with a rapier wit and an uncanny resemblance to Michelle Pfeiffer. "My 'job' from the day I got married was to be beautiful, to smile, and to always be a gracious hostess. Believe me, it was a full-time occupation, and I was good at it," she says. "Imagine my surprise when Jack did a Donald Trump and traded me in for a newer model with legs out to China and the IQ of a squid!" She laughs. "There I was, the rich divorcee, all dressed up with nowhere to go and nothing to do. So I played the stereotype to the hilt and went out and got my real estate license. And you know what? I'm making money—*my* money. And I'm feeling pretty damn proud of myself to boot."

Lucy and Ethel

The thought of entering the job market for the first time conjures up a priceless image from my absolutely favorite episode of "I Love Lucy." Remember when Lucy and Ethel decide to join the world of the gainfully employed and end up boxing bonbons in a candy factory? (As a perpetually chubby child, this was my life's dream, by the way!) Knowing nothing about candy packaging, they can't keep up with the quicker-than-lightning conveyor belt and end up eating the inventory rather than admit failure at the wrapping job!

It may be hard to shake the picture of yourself as being equally unqualified should you decide to enter the workplace. It might help to remember, though, that Lucy was only *acting* incompetent. Lucille Ball, by contrast, was one of the most successful actresses and businesswomen of her time. We're all great at convincing ourselves that we can't cut it, that we're destined for failure, but the trick is believing the opposite. And if you can't believe it, act as if you believe it. Your self-esteem has already ridden the divorce roller coaster. You've paid your dues, and now it's time to get off the ride. Gather your confidence, assess your skills, sell your abilities, and don't settle for less than you're worth.

Getting Down to Business

If you're feeling dubious about your "marketability" or you're just not sure what it is that you'd like to do, start by making a list of what you *can* do. Include "unofficial" jobs like keeping household financial records and balancing a budget. Consider special skills you may have and think about whether you could be a tennis instructor, give piano lessons, or teach a foreign language.

Also write down the things that you enjoy doing. Include

hobbies and activities you don't necessarily associate with work. Your doodles on the telephone message pad could lead you to a job illustrating books. Your cooking skills could take you into the catering field. And don't discount your skills as a homemaker. Martha Stewart has created quite a nice little business for herself, hasn't she?

It's a good idea to clean off a desk or designate a section of your dining room table as your job search "office." Keep all your notes and lists there as well as a typewriter or computer and a telephone. This way, whenever you're sitting at your desk, you're at work on your job search.

A big part of working on your job search involves the second D: discipline. Avoid the urge to turn on the TV. Stop yourself from making that tenth trip to the kitchen for yet another snack. And *don't* get back into bed.

You can do this.

Be Resourceful

Don't feel that you have to do this all on your own. Use your resources. Let your friends and relatives know that you're looking for a job. They may not be able to think of opportunities offhand, but you never know. You can also attend job seminars and networking events. And don't forget about some of the more traditional resources like employment agencies, executive search firms, and even the newspaper classified ads. Just because they're obvious doesn't mean they don't work.

You can also consider volunteering your time at the place where you'd like to work until a paid position opens up. I know for a fact that this method works because it's how I got my first paying job in my mid-twenties. I wasn't exactly thrilled at the prospect of being a volunteer because I really needed the money, but it was the only way they would consider hiring me. And let's just say that no one else was breaking down my door with job offers at the time. I spent six months writing an employee newsletter for free for a non-profit organization before I got my first paycheck.

That job ultimately led me to a career in the financial services industry and an opportunity to do something that I really love to do—educate women about money. So think of volunteering as an opportunity to get your foot in the door. You never know what's waiting for you behind that door.

PART V

• • •

Reentry

Living Single

● ● ●

In the immortal words of Yogi Berra (the real guy, not the bear), "It ain't over till it's over." Well, the good news is— it's over. Your divorce is final. Finito. End of story. No more depositions, no more accusations, no more financial wrangling. And the *very* good news is that now you can get on with the rest of your life.

That can be pretty scary stuff. At this point you may find yourself yo-yoing between profound relief and total panic. Yes, the divorce proceedings are finally over, but no, you don't exactly feel like singing, "I am woman, hear me roar." You may, in fact, feel downright exhausted, both emotionally and physically.

"The day my divorce became final, I didn't know what to do first—laugh, cry, or just crawl under the covers and never come out," remembers Julia, forty-seven and four years divorced. "It truly and honestly was the most confusing time of my life. For nearly seventeen months from start to finish, I lived and breathed that divorce. And after it was over, I didn't know what to do with myself."

Julia's solution was to start working on Julia—but not right away. First off, she stayed in bed for a solid week. "It took me that long to decide that it was even worth getting up in the morning," she says.

If Julia's "timeout" approach works for you, use it—without judgment and without recrimination. Whatever approach you take, this is the time to work on *you*. For perhaps the first time in a long time, you're in charge of your own life. You call the shots. That can be liberating, empowering, and also frightening.

It helps to focus on the possibilities instead of the pitfalls, and on the challenges instead of the crises.

Walk Slowly but Walk Tall

Congratulate yourself. You've finalized your settlement and have gotten through the hardest part of the divorce process. Or have you? Freedom sometimes seems like a mixed blessing. Sure, you can watch American Movie Classics every night instead of Letterman if you want. Who's going to stop you? But what if you end up watching old movies alone for the rest of your life? That's the ultimate scary script, isn't it?

Again, these fears are reasonable and normal. My divorced clients—even long after the event—recall the feeling of panic, the "who's going to take care of me now?" syndrome. Answer: You are going to take care of you.

You've already completed quite a journey. What began in legal discovery, followed by making list after list after list, has been finalized in a settlement agreement. You probably feel as though it's been nonstop decision making from the moment you first met with your attorney.

Now is the time to catch your breath. Now is the time to begin the process of rediscovering yourself—who you are as a person. Not as a wife, not as a mother—as you.

During her twenty-two-year marriage, my client Jennie had

grown accustomed to her husband always making their weekend plans. It was invariably either dinner with colleagues from his law firm, an evening at the theater, or a ballgame with the kids. Jennie wasn't used to filling her own social calendar, so in the months following her divorce, she found herself overwhelmed at the prospect of spending a Saturday night alone. Dinner with her ex's law firm buddies was definitely out. So was going to the ballgame with the kids because they were already at the ballgame with their father. And going to the theater all by herself was pitiful to the nth degree, she thought.

It took Jennie a good six months to get past her feeling of being ashamed of being alone. Going to the theater by herself *was* an option, she discovered. So was going with a friend, and so was staying home and renting a movie. In fact, almost anything and everything was an option now that Jennie was in charge of her own life.

She didn't make this discovery overnight, but she did make it. How? By learning to walk slowly in those first months after her divorce and also learning to walk tall.

Walking the Thin Line Between Your Emotions and Your Money

Now more than ever it's important to keep your emotions separate from your money. What's past is past. Unless your attorney feels that you have a reasonable expectation of revising your settlement or child support arrangements, my advice is to live with reality. Let it be. Turn any residual feelings of anger or resentment into positive energy. Get on with your life. Show the world and yourself that you can make it on your own.

This is not about being Mary Tyler Moore, it's about common sense. The consequences of not moving forward, of staying rooted in the past, will take a huge toll on your emotional well-being. It may also exact a high price financially.

"I'll admit it," says Evelyn, sixty-three, a gourmet vegetarian cook and gardening enthusiast. "For eleven years after my divorce, I wished every morning and every night for my ex to fall down a flight of stairs. And, believe me, it was all I could do not to go over to his office and push him myself," she says. "I believe to this day that he did me dirt in the settlement, but I'm tired of making myself sick about it. I spent thousands of dollars on three high-priced lawyers who all told me that it was a done deal, but I just couldn't let it go. I was making myself crazy, my kids crazy, and everyone around me crazy. I still don't forgive my ex, but I refuse to get irritated anymore. It's time to get on with my life."

This is also a time when your financial strength can fuel your emotional strength. If your financial house is in order and you're on the road to becoming financially independent, you won't feel so vulnerable emotionally. You won't feel as if you have to reach out to someone, anyone, for financial help no matter what the emotional cost to you.

And this dynamic comes full circle. As your emotional and financial strength builds, you'll begin to be ready for a new relationship. By coming from a position of strength and independence, you'll be able to evaluate more clearly whether this is really a healthy relationship for you.

What's Next?

You have already taken the property you received in your settlement agreement and begun managing it to your own maximum benefit. You've focused on implementing financial decisions that dovetail with your lifestyle decisions. As I mentioned in Part IV, some women choose investments that provide income while others choose to invest the bulk of their settlement dollars in a new house. Again, only you can evaluate what your needs are. Your "A team" can help you evaluate how you can use your settlement to meet those needs.

If you haven't already done so, you'll also want to devote

serious energy to putting your financial house in order. This is a critically important time to implement your new budget and to learn how to abide by it. Take a second (or third) look at your spending habits with an eye toward making positive changes so you'll have more money to save and invest.

As you learn to live with your new budget, you'll also learn to live with your child support payments. This may create single-parent issues that you have never had to deal with before. What do you do when your ex-husband takes your kids out to expensive dinners while your budget allows only pizza and an occasional Big Mac? Is this the shape of things to come? He's the hero; you're the zero?

And while you're knee deep trying to cope with single parenthood, how do you move forward with your own life? You've waded through umpteen documents, sat through countless meetings with your attorney, and worked your way through more boxes of Kleenex than you care to think about. You've gotten through your divorce. It's over. Now comes the real challenge: *Life!*

The initial logistics of getting your new life in order may seem like more than you can handle, but you *can* handle it. If you survived the divorce, you'll survive this. I promise.

Tying Up Loose Ends

You're just steps away from being home free. You're beginning to look forward, get organized, and get on with your life. But before you put your divorce completely behind you, you need to focus on tying up just a few more loose ends.

First of all, make sure that you have every part of your settlement agreement *in writing*. This includes provisions pertaining to property division, alimony, child support, custody arrangements, debt allocation, and anything else you and your ex-husband have agreed to. Even if your negotiations were amicable, don't rely on good faith. Get it in writing.

Know exactly what each of you owns and what each of you owes at the close of your divorce proceedings. You can't go on from here if you don't know where "here" is. So get your bearings first, then begin moving forward.

Getting Organized

Whether you prefer a stack of empty shoe boxes or a sturdy metal file cabinet—I vote for the file cabinet—now is the time to designate some storage space specifically for all documents, letters, records, and other paperwork relating to your final divorce decree. This will include records of alimony and child support payments made by your ex as well as records from the sale of any property that you received in your settlement.

Once you have your final judgment and your settlement agreement in hand, you should make several copies. Keep the originals in a safety deposit box, one copy in your divorce file, and another copy in your desk for easy reference. Your lawyer should also have a copy on file. If you never have to look at it again, fine. If you do, you'll know exactly where it is.

Is It a Done Deal?

Even though your settlement is the final product of what may have seemed like endless negotiations, it is not always etched in stone. Sometimes a done deal can get undone—but only if you and your ex-husband *both* agree to change the terms of your settlement. In real life this doesn't happen very often.

My client Sylvia agreed to what she felt was a generous settlement offer, only to find out six months later that her husband's privately owned company was being taken public. In plain English, he stands to benefit by several million dollars; she gets zippity-doodah. Naturally, Sylvia feels it's only fair to renegotiate her settlement. Her ex-husband is of a different opinion. Now it's back to the lawyers for both of them.

Unless her husband miraculously sees the error of his ways and offers Sylvia her fair share, she will have to go to court with new evidence to support her request for a renegotiation of her settlement agreement. The burden of proof is on her. If she can't convince the judge otherwise, she'll have to live with the original deal, like it or not. And, believe me, she *won't* like it!

It's All in the Details

Familiarize yourself with each and every item you received in your divorce settlement. If you own it now, make sure it's yours and yours alone. Anything that is still listed in both your names should be changed to reflect your sole ownership as soon as possible. Contact the Department of Motor Vehicles to change the ownership on your car. You can change the title to any real estate that you received by going to the county recorder's office. And don't forget to meet with your investment adviser, broker, or banker to make sure that your stocks, bonds, mutual funds, and other securities are held in your name only. If they were previously held as joint property, you will need a letter of authorization from your husband to transfer ownership.

If you have not already done so, update your will or trust document to reflect current events. Do you still want to leave all your money to your husband now that he's your ex-husband? No? Then plan on a visit to your estate attorney sooner rather than later.

Protecting Your Credit

What if your ex-husband agreed to pay some or all of your joint debts as part of the divorce settlement? Are you off the hook financially? Not by a long shot. If he doesn't honor his commitment, you could be liable. Contact your creditors and let them know that it is your ex-husband's obligation to repay them, but ask them to notify you in writing if payments aren't being made in a timely manner. You need to protect your own credit. It doesn't make sense to see your credit rating go down the drain because your ex-husband is negligent. Even if it means paying the bills yourself and going to court to demand reimbursement from your ex, do it. It isn't fair, it purely stinks, but it may be the only way to protect yourself.

Reentry is about cutting any lingering ties to the past, but it *isn't* about cutting off your nose to spite your face. Don't teach your ex-husband a lesson at the cost of getting a failing grade on your own credit report.

Your Settlement Portfolio: When to Hold 'em, When to Fold 'em

Now that you've received your final settlement, it's time to take another look at what you have. In Part IV you determined what you need your money to do for you, now and in the future, by focusing on your short- and long-term financial goals. If you're lucky, the assets you received will go a long way toward meeting those goals.

Now that you are the sole owner of your post-divorce assets, sit down with your certified financial planner or stockbroker and review every investment in your portfolio. Do you understand what you own? Do you have the right mix of stocks, bonds, and cash? Do your investments reflect your financial goals and your risk tolerance? If not, now is the time to make changes.

Now is also the time to get rid of those investments that you never thought made sense in the first place. Maybe your ex bought them over your objection, or maybe you bought them yourself and have been holding on forever, hoping they would go up or break even. Does it make sense to keep on holding them, or does it make more sense to realign your portfolio to meet your current needs?

When you're deciding what part of your portfolio to keep, remember that you don't have to make changes just for the sake of making changes. Just because you're no longer married to your husband doesn't mean that everything you invested in together has to go out the window right along with him. Don't get rid of a good thing out of anger or frustration at your ex. That would be the ultimate act of cutting off your nose to spite your face.

On the flip side, don't feel compelled to keep an investment that isn't working for you anymore. Sentimental attachments are fine, but they have no place in the financial world. If it works for you, keep it. If it doesn't, get rid of it.

Risk and the Two C's and Two D's

When it comes to managing money, women tend to be much more risk averse than men. That's not terribly surprising when you consider that the world of investing is often new territory for women. It's natural to exercise caution when you're not sure what lies ahead.

For many recently divorced women, though, this natural caution can evolve into downright fear—to the extent of experiencing what I call the "bag lady nightmares" even when they're fully awake. In the early months following their divorce, these women worry that one false move is going to land them on the street, all alone without a dime. And this fear cuts across all socioeconomic lines. I've heard about bag lady nightmares even from women who received multimillion-dollar settlements. Are their fears real? From a strictly financial perspective, no; from an emotional and psychological perspective, absolutely.

Laura, fifty-two, a schoolteacher who retired after teaching tenth-grade algebra for nearly twenty-seven years, is "scared to death of losing money." Divorced eighteen months ago, she received nearly a million dollars and a mortgage-free house as part of her settlement. That should go a long way toward making her feel financially secure, right? Try telling that to Laura.

"I don't even want to hear about stocks and bonds," she says. "I won't take *any* risk. My money is staying strictly in Treasuries or CDs. I don't care if it makes sense or not. This money is all I have and probably all I'll ever have, and I won't risk it," she insists.

In this case, Laura's comfort level is clearly dictating her investment strategy. Her fear of losing money supersedes my first D, diversification, and even to some extent my first C, common sense.

As a financial professional, my job is to explain to Laura that what she perceives as a risk-free investment strategy carries risk—most notably, purchasing power risk. While Laura says that she doesn't want to lose money, she *is* losing money—in this case, to inflation and taxes.

Like Laura, you may be allowing bag lady nightmares to rule your investment decisions at the moment. Don't worry about it. Thankfully, in most instances this tendency is short-lived. Over time, excessive panic generally gives way to prudent caution.

As you learn more about investing and more about the concept of risk versus reward, chances are you'll stretch your comfort level to accommodate your common sense and your need for diversification. The goal here is not to feel comfortable investing in pork belly futures. It's to understand the difference between taking a risk and taking a flyer.

Minimizing Risk: The Chicken Approach

Let's say you're at the point where you're comfortable taking some risk but not a lot of risk. You've decided to add some stocks to your portfolio but aren't sure how to go about buying them. Should you plunk your money down now and hope for the best or wait a few months and see if the stock market tumbles because then maybe you can buy them cheaper? Good question. The answer, of course, depends on whether stocks are headed higher or lower. That's an even better question!

Because no one has the answer to that one, you might want to try using my chicken approach to investing. Don't bother trying to guess which way the market is headed. Don't be a bull *or* a bear—be a chicken. Invest half your money now and the other half three to six months from now. If your stocks go up, you'll have a profit on the first half; if they go down, you'll buy the rest at a lower price. Not a bad way to split the difference.

My chicken approach also works very well in reverse. Let's say you've held on to an investment for a while and now you have a tidy profit. You're not sure what to do. Do you sell now or wait to see if it goes higher? And what if you don't sell and it goes lower?

I've said to clients many times over the years and it's worth repeating here: Bulls and bears make money, pigs get slaughtered. Again, try being a chicken.

Sell half your shares and keep the other half. That way you've locked in a profit on at least part of your investment. If it keeps going up, great. And if it goes down, you still have money in your pocket from selling the first half. Not a bad deal all around.

Timing Isn't Everything

There are two schools of thought when it comes to making money in the stock market. One advocates a "buy and hold" approach, and the other attempts to "time" the market by identifying highs and lows and investing accordingly. The key to being a successful market timer is being able to spot the highs and lows—an inexact science at best.

Which path should you follow? The path of common sense. Over the last forty years, stock prices have gone up in all but nine years. That means that if you did nothing but buy and hold your stocks, you'd certainly have made money. Timing the market, on the other hand, leaves you vulnerable to buying and selling at the wrong time. If your timing was off during the last forty years and you missed out on the best years for stock market gains, you also missed out on some very significant profits.

The moral of the story is that you're much better off staying the course with a buy-and-hold strategy than timing the market and missing the boat altogether.

Buyer Beware

Always trust your instincts and let your own good common sense guide you. And don't let other people sabotage you. This isn't paranoia talking, it's reality. There *is* someone out there who is waiting to take advantage of you. It's not always the obviously shady-looking guy with two days' growth of beard on his face. It could be a smooth-talking salesman or business manager or even a long-lost boyfriend whom you haven't seen since high school.

If you don't take charge of your money and make your own financial decisions, there are plenty of people out there who will be more than happy to do it for you—much to your detriment. It's sad but true. The important thing is to avoid looking to other people for easy answers. And if you're prepared to take responsibility for your own finances, *you* won't look like a target to Mr. Slick.

Take a lesson from my client Dorothy, a self-proclaimed "little old lady from Pasadena," who is nobody's fool. After her divorce at age sixty-three, Dorothy decided that she wanted a smaller car and was deciding between a Mazda and a Toyota. On her fourth visit to the showroom, the Mazda salesman thought he could close the deal by using a little psychology. He told Dorothy that she was obviously afraid of making a commitment, that this was a big step and it scared her, and that she could trust him to make the right decision for her. According to Dorothy, he actually did make the decision for her. His attitude convinced her to walk right out of that showroom and never come back. (P.S. She decided that she didn't like the Toyota salesman's attitude, either, and ended up buying a Buick!)

Do It Yourself

Dorothy was pleased as punch at making her own decisions. After forty-three years of marriage to a demanding and overbearing husband, she loved the freedom and independence of being on her own. You may feel otherwise. "I'm planning to remarry. I'll just let my new husband take care of the money," you say. Or you may think it's too late in life to start learning how to be moneysmart.

Here's why I disagree: As far as I'm concerned, whether you're single forever or plan to remarry tomorrow, whether you're twentysomething or eightysomething, it's still important to be financially self-sufficient.

You may think you'll feel an enormous sense of relief if you hand over responsibility for managing your finances to someone else. But what starts out as stress relief can turn into high anxiety very quickly if your new husband mismanages your funds and you end up watching your money evaporate before your eyes. It certainly isn't good for your sense of security or self-esteem to feel like a sitting duck, hoping no one rips you off or sends you to the poorhouse. And it's also not good for you to wait for the next man in your life to take care of you. Prince Charming II? Have we learned nothing?

Always keep a firm grasp on your common sense, and don't let it be overruled by your need to be taken care of. Feeling vulnerable and acting vulnerable are two different things. Inside you may be screaming, "I don't know what I'm doing." But the view from the outside needs to be, "Don't mess with me, I know what's up."

That goes for family members, too. If you suddenly feel pressured to cough up money for a relative's surefire investment or an emergency loan, let your common sense rule. This doesn't mean ignoring your family or being indifferent to their needs. It just means being careful and thinking with your head as well as your heart.

Remember the Taxman

No matter what month it is, it always seems as if April 15 is just around the corner, so as you think about money strategies, keep a close eye on the taxman.

The laws have recently changed—yet again. Personal exemptions for certain taxpayers have been permanently phased out, and business meals are now only 50 percent deductible, as opposed to 80 percent in years past. That may make a substantial difference to you, or it may mean nothing at all. Find out how the new changes will affect your tax bill, and do so well in advance of next April 15.

If you decide to go into business for yourself, learn about self-employment taxes and understand how estimated income tax payments work. It's not worth paying a penalty when a little education can get your tax house in order.

A Penny Saved

I've talked a lot about budgeting. For most people, this is considerably less fun than cleaning out the garage, so it tends to get shunted to the very bottom of the to-do list.

Post-divorce, budgeting becomes a huge priority for most women and scoots right up to the top of the "I hate this, but I have to do it" list. Figuring out where you spend money unnecessarily and looking for less expensive alternatives is an important first step in learning how to cut costs.

One of the less obvious ways to cut costs involves evaluating your health, automobile, and property insurance. Do some comparison shopping. Find out if you're paying the lowest rates available for comparable coverage or if there are better alternatives. Even if you retain your current policies, it may make sense to opt for higher deductibles in exchange for significantly lower premium payments.

Closer to the home front, there are several effective and very practical ways to stretch your budget and cut costs. Buying in bulk is one of them. I used to shudder at the thought of buying bulk groceries. No way, not me. I wouldn't be caught dead lugging an industrial-strength box of Tide down the grocery aisle. But when I figured out that bulk buying means making fewer trips to the supermarket, it seemed like a monumental waste of time *and* money not to. And—would you believe it?—today it's chic to be thrifty. People I know no longer brag about how much they spent on something; they can't wait to tell you how much they saved. There's even a five-and-dime store called "Thrifty of Beverly Hills." *Très* trendy!

Creative Cost Cutting

There's no doubt in anyone's mind that no matter how politically correct saving money may be, it just isn't as much fun as spending money, right? Wrong! When we cut back on our family entertainment budget last year, my three sons—the champion spenders of the West Coast—discovered that having a good time didn't necessarily have to cost a bundle. We could see the latest "hot" movie at the bargain-priced twilight show instead of paying nearly double to see it just three hours later. And we could recycle the gazillion empty soda cans in the basement, using the proceeds to enjoy a dinner out instead of ordering pizza in.

Be creative! Invite friends over for a potluck dinner. Everyone brings something different and gets to enjoy one another's cooking and company without breaking the bank.

Debt: You Can Take the Girl out of Cleveland, But . . .

I've lived in Southern California for nearly twenty-two years now, much of that time in the financial fantasyland of Beverly Hills. But my money values were born and bred in Cleveland, Ohio, in the early 1950s. And to this day I have what may be considered a decidedly midwestern approach to debt: Don't spend what you don't have.

Common sense to me, radical thinking to others. It surely isn't what credit card companies will tell you. And it may not be what your cousin Ralph who has a great "sure thing" business opportunity will tell you. But let *me* tell you what I learned at my grandmother's knee: Avoid debt like the plague. Thinking back, I don't remember Grandma ever owning a credit card in her life.

There are some situations, of course, when taking on debt is virtually unavoidable. Few people can purchase a home outright, but there's a world of difference between taking out a long-term loan to buy a house whose value will likely appreciate over time and taking on credit card debt to finance a discretionary purchase that you could probably live without.

First of all, unlike interest on home mortgage payments, interest on credit card debt is *not* deductible. It's also expensive. Credit card companies typically charge 15 percent to 20 percent or more annual interest on unpaid balances. That can get way up into the thousands for people with high credit limits. And make no mistake about it: Once you start charging up a storm, your credit card company will gladly extend your limit so you can buy more—and owe more. That's how they make money, and that's how you get into trouble.

My advice is to live very close to your means. Think about curtailing your lifestyle *before* you think about incurring debt. Unless it causes you physical or emotional hardship, you're much better off not spending what you don't have. Especially in the early days following your divorce, it's better to err on the side of caution. Know exactly how far your money will stretch before you risk writing a check that will come bouncing right back at you.

A Necessary Evil

If you do have to go into debt, do your homework first. Interest rates and annual fees on credit cards can vary substantially, so it's definitely worth doing some comparison shopping.

You may need to use a credit card to help amortize a major purchase like a personal computer to start a home-based business. If you're unable to pay for it in full at the outset, buying on credit will allow you to get your business started while you pay for your computer over the next several months. But avoid letting that debt linger on your credit card statement month after month, accruing more and more interest for you to pay. Set up a disciplined but realistic payment schedule and stick to it until the bill is marked "paid in full."

The best way to avoid having to dig yourself out of a financial hole is to be aware of your personal pitfalls. Be honest about your spending habits. I know that I have a particular weakness for "free gift with purchase" offers. My friend Sharon never met a lipstick that she didn't like. And some women go on a spending spree every time they get a paycheck.

"It's like the money is burning a hole in my pocket, and I just have to buy *something,*" says Melinda, thirty-three, a fiery redhead with sea-green eyes, and a reformed spendaholic. "I finally had to have my paycheck on 'direct deposit' to my checking account. If I don't ever see the money or hold it in my hand, I don't spend it nearly as fast. I don't know why it works, but it works," she says. Melinda would do well to consider an automatic monthly investment plan in a good stock mutual fund as well. That way the money she is *not* spending can be growing into quite a tidy sum.

If you're meeting your saving goals and have all your monthly bills paid, it's fine to indulge yourself occasionally. But if your spending habits consistently get you into trouble, learn to recognize the potholes in the road and make a conscious effort to steer around them. By knowing your weaknesses, you can keep them from sabotaging your finances.

Bringing Home the Bacon and Frying It Up in a Pan

Remember that Enjoli perfume commercial that aired several years ago? The heroine was a combination superexecutive/supermom/supersexy Renaissance woman of the 80s. She brought home the bacon and fried it up in a pan—still dressed in her perfectly elegant, cool-as-a-cucumber silk suit. Yeah, right! Is there a woman alive who lives this version of reality? I don't think so. Except maybe in the Twilight Zone!

For single mothers, especially those who work full-time

outside the home, reality is more like sweatpants, hamburgers, and after-dinner primal screaming in the shower. Juggling home and hearth and kids and work is the ultimate exercise in time—to say nothing of stress—management.

Take chauffeuring the kids to school, for example. Maybe during your marriage you could count on your husband to pick the children up from school in the afternoon. Unless he continues to do so as part of your custody arrangement, you may have to change your work schedule so you can pick them up yourself. Or better yet, you can try to arrange a carpool. Either way, it's a challenge—and a far cry from Enjoli-land!

Supporting Your Children

The trauma of going through a divorce, regardless of how amicable it may be, takes its toll on you and certainly on your children. Supporting your children through this difficult time will require all your emotional energy at a time when your own reserves may be running on empty.

Let's talk about the financial reality first since, in some respects, it may be more manageable than the emotional fallout.

After you receive your court order, you'll have an agreement stipulating how much child support your husband will pay you each month and when the payments will be made. Be sure to get this agreement in writing, including provisions for visitation rights. File it carefully with your other post-divorce documents.

You should also keep a meticulous record of all child support payments that you receive, so you can establish a pattern of behavior. Take note if the payments are consistently late or always short by $50, $100, and so forth. Record the date that the payment is due, the date that it is actually received, the amount due, and the amount received.

Along with the record of payments, you should also consider keeping a log of child-related expenses. This will be useful if you need to go back to your husband or back to court to ask for more money. If you can document the fact that your children's expenses consistently exceed your ex-husband's child support payments, you may stand a better chance of getting an increase.

It is common for ex-husbands to resent making payments, especially if they feel that they don't get to spend as much time with their children as they'd like to. Try not to add fuel to that fire. Don't bad-mouth him to your children or refuse to let them see him. Getting angry and getting even aren't worth the risk of his refusing to make his support payments. This isn't about appeasing him, it's about protecting your children.

If, on the other hand, you need to seek enforcement because your husband is either consistently late or is refusing to make payments altogether, don't hesitate to take action. This, too, is about protecting your children. You can go to an attorney or to a child support enforcement agency, or you can try to settle the matter yourself by communicating directly with your ex. Don't wait to take action until you can barely scrape by. As soon as you see the handwriting on the wall, deal with it. Nip it in the bud before it gets worse. If you can settle things between the two of you, great. If not, go to court.

Visitation

When you arrange for visitation, it's important to establish a set schedule. Both of you have to agree that you'll stick to it, no matter what. In general, most parents arrange for the non-custodial parent (usually the father) to have the children every other weekend and some holidays. Whatever you decide, be consistent. It's a lot easier on your children if they don't feel they're being shuttled between the two of you at random. If they understand that there's a set schedule, they won't feel unloved and neglected when Dad doesn't take them out during the week. They'll know he's waiting to see them on the weekend. It saves a lot of confusion and a lot of hurt feelings.

Time to Be a Single Parent

Unless you've always had sole responsibility for taking care of your children and your husband never lifted a finger to help, you'll probably find that raising kids as a single parent takes up a lot of your time and energy. Now you're the one who takes the kids to the dentist, goes shopping for shoes, helps them with their homework, holds them when they cry, wakes them up in the morning, and tucks them in at night. In short, you're doing it all. And doing the job of two parents all by yourself takes creativity, careful planning, and a great deal of patience. More than anything else, though, it takes getting past the resentment that often goes hand in hand with being a single mom.

You may have good reason to feel resentful. It's no picnic seeing your ex-husband doing all the fun stuff with the kids on the weekends while you're stuck dragging them to the orthodontist and the pediatrician for flu shots. Great association they're making, huh? Dad equals fun, Mom equals a pain in the butt.

When you're the custodial parent, you're also the one supervising after-school homework sessions, and limiting after-dinner television time. And you're the one who is handy when, at nine o'clock at night, your ten-year-old remembers that he volunteered to bring brownies to the school bake sale tomorrow. So even if you and your ex-husband have agreed to share some tasks like carpool duty, as the resident parent you'll still end up with most of the child-related responsibilities.

Is that fair? Maybe not. But ask yourself the pivotal question: Is it worth it? Would you rather live with the unfairness, or would you rather live without your children—except on weekends and holidays? It's a package deal with no free lunch.

Bearing the Emotional Burden

Being a single parent often involves dealing with a whole new set of highly charged emotional issues. It also sometimes means bearing the brunt of your children's anger and frustration. Kids blame the parent who will accept the blame, and usually that's Mom, whether it's her fault or not. It's also the mother who's mostly on the receiving end of their acting out and their hostility. They may feel powerless because they had no say in the matter. No one asked the kids if they thought it was a good idea for Mom and Dad to split up. They were probably told after the fact, yet their lives were profoundly affected by the divorce. So now they'll take every opportunity to exert any little bit of power they can get their hands on. And usually the custodial parent, typically the mother, becomes the most convenient target.

Children of all ages have some unique form of expressing their frustration, upset, and anger. A toddler will cry or start wetting the bed. Teenagers may respond by acting out in class, getting careless about schoolwork, or breaking curfew.

And it's not only young children who react to their parents' divorce with shock and anger. For adult children, seeing Mom and Dad get divorced after thirty years of marriage rocks their whole world, too. And you'll hear about it—very loudly and in no uncertain terms.

If your ex-husband won't talk about your divorce with your children, the responsibility will fall entirely on you to explain why Mom and Dad no longer live under the same roof. You're the one who has to reassure them that your divorce has nothing to do with them, that you and their father still love them just as much as you always did. These things need to be said, but when you're left holding the bag, it's hard not to feel like a criminal being cross-examined on a witness stand. Your kids may look at you and ask, "What did you do to make Daddy leave?" and suddenly you're forced to defend yourself for something that isn't even your fault.

This can be emotionally draining and incredibly frustrating. Your natural inclination may be to paint their father as the bad guy—especially if he is. Don't do it. It will hurt them more than it does him. But don't let yourself be the fall guy, either. And don't take the rap for anything that he did. Encourage your children to discuss their feelings with their father, not just with you. Kids aren't stupid. They know the score, and they usually know the truth. Let them deal with their father in their own way. Love them and protect them, but give them some room.

Resisting Emotional Blackmail

I said earlier that children often feel powerless when their parents divorce. One of the more unpleasant ways kids try to regain a sense of power is by playing one parent off against the other and using emotional blackmail to get what they want. Be aware that even the best, most well-adjusted kids play this game. They may treat you badly, blame you, and even threaten to go live with their father if you don't "shape up." Be prepared for this. Forewarned is forearmed.

When you're divorced, your kids quickly figure out which parent is more likely to say yes to a specific request. You'll say no to a movie on a school night, and before you know it, your daughter bounces back with the age-old battle cry: "But Daddy said I could!"

Kids are also very perceptive when it comes to spotting particular pressure points. Sometimes they know just where to get you. Then asking Dad about the movies also becomes a way of getting back at Mom—usually for some imagined injustice.

Of course, the ultimate power trip for a kid is threatening to go live with Dad if you don't give in to her demand du jour. My client, Josie, finally had enough of this. "Fine, go live with your father," she said, and off stomped her twelve-year-old daughter to do just that.

"Are you really going to let her go?" I asked.

"With pleasure," said Josie. "I won't be held hostage, and I won't be threatened. If Lisa can live by the rules, fine. If not, she can go live with her dad and threaten him." That's just what Lisa proceeded to do for the next three months until *both* parents put a stop to it.

Even if you and your ex-husband aren't exactly on good terms, the best thing you can do to combat being manipulated by your children is to stay on the same page as parents. Try to come to a workable agreement about how child-rearing decisions will be handled. Then stick to the agreement no matter what.

Dealing with Guilt

I have only one thing to say about guilt: Forget about it. Believe me, I've been worked over by the master guilt mongers of the universe. (They should live and be well to 120.) Today, I decline to be made to feel guilty about anything. No kidding—I mean it. For me, feeling guilty is something I just don't indulge in anymore. I do the best I can and leave it at that.

A great way to avoid guilt is to concentrate on being honest. Don't try to put one over on your kids, and don't try to hide the truth. Usually, they'll find out anyway and resent you for not being straight with them.

When it comes to sticking to your household budget, explain to your kids that you're not saying no just to be mean. Be honest with them and tell them what's going on. If money is tight right now, you may have no choice but to say no to special treats. They'll come to understand that saying "we can't afford it" isn't fun for you, either. I find offering an alternative helps. If you can't afford Disneyland, how about the video arcade?

Be honest with them about your social life, too. If you start dating someone, it's natural for your kids to be less than thrilled. Anyone you bring home will be seen as a barrier to your getting back together with Dad—even if Dad is engaged to someone else. You may know that your divorce was final, but in the hearts and minds of your children, that doesn't mean anything. They're still cheering for Mom and Dad. Even if your new beau is the nicest guy in the world, chances are slim to none that they'll like him. They may give him the cold shoulder or show open hostility. And they may take it out on you as well. Allow them this. Just as you're entitled to date, your kids are entitled to dislike the person you're dating. Respect their rights but insist that they respect yours as well.

Who's the Parent Here?

Occasionally, we all need a shoulder to cry on and a friendly ear to listen to our tales of woe. That's what friends are for. But that's *not* what kids are for. Unfortunately, some parents fall into the dangerous habit of airing their emotional laundry at home, loudly and repeatedly. It's not fair to put your kids in the position of having to be your therapist. It's your child's right to expect unequivocal love and support from you. There is a limit, however, to what you can expect from your child.

By definition, the parent-child relationship is an unequal one. Don't expect mutuality, because there's nothing even-steven about it. You are your children's caregiver; they're not yours. If you sit at the dinner table every night and discuss your problems ad infinitum, your child may inadvertently start to take on a parenting role. Kids grow up quickly enough. Don't rush them into it. Inevitably there comes a time when children do take care of their parents, but don't make that time come any sooner than it has to.

You don't have to go to the opposite extreme and hide your feelings from your children, either. It's okay to tell them how you feel. And if you're vulnerable or lonely, it's okay to let your kids see that, too. You're not made of stone, and you shouldn't pretend to be. But know where to draw the line. Don't expect your child to be your friend, confidante, or therapist—just your child.

Respect Your Own Needs

While it's true your job is to be a parent to your children, you have the absolute right to expect your kids to understand your needs, too—for space, time, privacy, and, most of all, to be your own person. Don't give them everything you have and leave nothing for yourself.

There will be times when you'll feel like your coping skills are at an all-time low. It's okay to let your children know when you're at the end of your rope. They'll find out soon enough anyway.

If you're the one who initiated the divorce, your kids may think they're the only ones who are unhappy that Dad's gone. They often have the mistaken impression that since you're the one who wanted the divorce, you must be happy now that it's over. Well, maybe you're glad to be done with the depositions and the reams of paperwork, but that doesn't mean you feel like jumping for joy.

There will be times when you feel downright blue. That's normal. Your kids need to learn that seeing you upset just means you're human, that you have feelings, too. They need to learn how to be supportive of you. That's different from taking care of you or providing a free counseling session. It's a basic level of understanding.

There's no question that sometimes it feels good to indulge yourself in a good, thorough wallow. You can't be expected to keep it together all the time. But know when enough is enough. At a certain point you have to suit up, show up, and do what you have to do.

Prince Charming and Other Fairy Tales

I've talked a lot about financial strategies, about the importance of establishing credit in your own name, and about how to give the job market a good run for its money. My goal here is to help you become a financially independent woman. Whether you choose to remain single indefinitely or remarry immediately, achieving that goal will stand you in good stead for the rest of your life.

Many women say that while they cherish their newfound independence post-divorce, they still secretly dream of being rescued by a Robert Redford look-alike and living happily ever after. And after all those months of legal wrangling and emotional wear and tear, I can certainly appreciate how the life of a fairy tale princess might seem appealing—but they don't call it a fairy tale for nothing. For most women, being rescued by a handsome young prince and living happily ever after just isn't going to happen. (Ask Princess Diana if you don't believe me.) That's not to say that you can't enjoy a wonderful, new relationship with another man. Just don't mistake him for Prince Charming—who, by the way, was a great kisser but couldn't balance a checkbook for beans!

The Second Time Around

You're a single woman now, but chances are that you won't be single forever. And you may not even be single for long. On average, divorced women who remarry typically do so within about three and a half years after their divorce. For women over forty, the average interval between divorce and remarriage is a little longer—about six years.

Nearly two-thirds of all divorced men and women marry someone who is also divorced. And they often bring a lot of emotional and financial baggage along with them. If your ex-husband handled all the family finances in your first marriage, you may be tempted to repeat this pattern in your second marriage. Don't do it. After all the time and hard work you've put into learning how to be financially independent, don't you owe it to yourself to preserve that independence and let it flourish? Why not form a financial partnership where both of you can share financial responsibility and make decisions together? The best moneysmart marriages are always based on this kind of sharing and mutual respect.

Prenuptial Agreements

Does forming a financial partnership necessitate commingling all your financial assets—effectively turning "my" money and "your" money into "our" money? Not by a longshot. One of the most important times to keep your emotions separate from your money is when you're thinking about starting a new life with a new man. If anything, your divorce has certainly taught you the value of staying in control of your financial life. Don't risk losing your settlement—or, worse, your future security—by failing to protect yourself with a prenuptial agreement in the event that your second marriage doesn't work out. You may be afraid of jeopardizing your new love relationship, but you should be even more concerned about jeopardizing your own future.

Here's a scenario that I encounter all too often: A client receives a substantial settlement from her first marriage and begins investing it using her own financial goals and the Two C's and Two D's as guidelines. So far, so good. Several years go by, and she meets and decides to marry a man who has far less money than she, reasoning that she has enough for both of them. He's warm, loving, sensitive, and everything she wants in a husband. And because she doesn't want to "insult" him by talking about money, she doesn't raise the issue of a prenuptial agreement. They're getting ready to share a life together, and the last thing she wants to talk about is what happens if the marriage doesn't work out.

That's all well and good as long as the marriage *does* work out. But if it doesn't, she'll wish that she had thought longer and harder about doing a prenup.

What Is a Prenup?

With the growing number of divorced men and women in the United States, the practice of signing prenups is also growing as more people realize that marriage is an economic partnership as well as a love relationship.

A prenuptial agreement is a document signed before your marriage that specifies how your assets will be divided in the event of a separation, divorce, or the death of a spouse. It can also outline how the family finances will be handled during your marriage.

For a prenuptial pact to hold up to legal scrutiny, it must disclose all assets, income, and liabilities that you and your future husband have before you marry. That way each of you knows exactly what is at stake and what you may be giving up if the marriage should end. The agreement must also be signed voluntarily by both of you. If one person signs under threat or duress, the agreement isn't valid.

Will He Think I Don't Love Him?

Prenups are not a sign that you don't love your husband-to-be or that you don't have faith that the marriage will last. It just means that you're thinking with your head as well as your heart. If you've spent many agonizing months hammering out a divorce settlement, it makes sense to think twice before getting in bed financially with someone else.

For women who have children, prenups are especially important because they can safeguard the children's trust funds, inheritances, or monies that have been set aside for their college education. If your future husband has children from a previous marriage, your prenuptial agreement can also delineate how his children's expenses will be paid—by him separately or by both of you together.

If you're considering marrying a man with fewer assets than you or with much more debt, a prenup is critical. A written agreement signed by both of you before the marriage will make crystal clear which assets and which liabilities belong to each partner. You certainly don't want to get stuck paying off your new husband's two-year-old MasterCard debt, especially if the charges were run up by his ex-wife.

Commingling Assets

My advice about commingling assets is simple: Don't do it! The hazard of commingling your money with his is that you risk losing the divorce settlement that you've just worked so hard to get. If the marriage doesn't work out with husband number two and your assets are commingled, what's yours now could be his later.

Commingling assets doesn't just mean putting your money and his money in the same bank account. It can also mean adding his name to the title on your house or as a joint tenant on your investment portfolio. Any way you slice it, though, it's not a good idea.

Still, some women do it anyway. Why? The most common reason that my clients give for commingling assets the second time around is that it's a show of good faith. A woman may think that if she brings up the subject of a prenuptial agreement, it's like saying the marriage is doomed before it starts. Or she *does* bring it up and gets the argument, "You wouldn't ask me to do this if you really loved me," from the man she plans to marry. Her response at that point becomes: "I do love you, so if you don't feel comfortable with this, let's just forget about it. It's not that important."

This is an accident waiting to happen. And a situation that rarely happens in reverse.

When men ask women to sign prenuptial agreements, they view it as good business, not as a test of love. Women, however, often get tied up in emotional knots over what's basically a financial agreement. You can love your husband-to-be and still ask him to sign a prenup. Love and money aren't mutually exclusive.

"Andy knows I just love him to bits," says Georgia, forty-eight, with a southern drawl to match her name. "Even so, he knows I won't marry him if he doesn't sign on the dotted line. I gave away half of everything I owned when my first husband and I got divorced five years ago, and every penny was mine to begin with. As much as I love Andy—and I *do* love him—I will never make that mistake again. What's mine," says Georgia, "stays mine."

You have to listen to your warm fuzzies, of course, and do what feels right for you. If you decide to commingle your assets, that's your choice. Just make sure that you understand what's at risk. Know going into the marriage how many dollars will be walking out of the marriage along with husband number two if things don't work out between you. If you can live with it, fine. Just run the numbers first. It's important to know exactly how much is at stake before you make a decision that may affect the rest of your life.

Postnuptial Agreements

Another growing trend that parallels the changing face of marriage and divorce in this country is the evolution of the postnuptial agreement. This is a document written and signed by both of you after you're already married. Like a prenup, the function of a postnup is to outline who gets what in the event of divorce. Postnups are generally used to address financial issues that weren't addressed before the marriage. Think of them almost as prenups after the fact.

A postnuptial agreement can also be written in the event that one partner receives a large sum of money during the marriage. If you're the beneficiary of your grandfather's multimillion-dollar estate, for example, you can draw up a postnuptial agreement specifically stating that you're entitled to keep your entire inheritance should you divorce even if the funds have been commingled during your marriage.

Financially Happily Ever After

Whether you have a prenup, a postnup, or no nup, the key to living financially happily ever after lies in feeling confident and moneysmart.

For many women their divorce is the defining event of their lives. It can be a painful odyssey that haunts you for the rest of your days, or it can be an open doorway to a new and better place.

Speaking of her own divorce, former California State Treasurer Kathleen Brown says: "Probably the most important thing it did for me is make me realize how vulnerable we all are in life and how much we have to take responsibility for ourselves." She describes her divorce as an "epiphany," claiming that it gave her "a very strong personal desire to have independence and to be smart about areas of financial management."

She wasn't kidding around, either.

Kathleen's determination to gain financial knowledge and independence in her personal life blossomed into a successful career as chief financial officer of one of the largest states in the country.

Now how's that for a happy ending?

Conclusion:
There Is Life After Divorce

You've done it. You've made it through the months of financial wrangling and last-minute legal maneuvers. You've survived the tears, the accusations, the fits of anger, and the countless words of unsolicited advice from well-meaning (and some not-so-well-meaning) friends and relatives.

As you go on from here, you know that your life will never be the same. But take heart—*and keep moving forward!*

For most divorced and divorcing women, the breakup of a marriage does not have to be a road map to financial and social gloom and doom. Quite the contrary.

Divorce hurts, but it also makes most women stronger—and happier.

Describing the dissolution of her thirty-year marriage as "the greatest loss of my life," silver-haired former Texas governor Ann Richards, now a senior adviser at a high-powered Washington law firm, says, "I dealt with it by telling myself that now I had an opportunity to do things that I would not have had an opportunity to do if I had stayed married."[14]

Life after divorce is, indeed, about identifying opportunities, making choices, and embracing change. Most of all, it's about letting go of the past.

Don't worry about what you could have done differently last month, last year, or even ten years ago. Why look over your shoulder when you can spend the same time and energy investing in your future? Yesterday's money mistakes have nothing to do with your ability to be moneysmart today.

Now it's your turn to live your life: to discover who you are and what's important to you, to stand on your own two feet and take care of yourself.

It's your turn to shine.

Sources

1. *American Demographics,* October 1988.
2. *Statistical Handbook on Women in America,* compiled and edited by Cynthia Taeuber, 1991.
3. National Center for Retirement Research.
4. National Center for Retirement Research.
5. *Statistical Handbook on Women in America,* compiled and edited by Cynthia Taeuber, 1991.
6. National Center for Retirement Research.
7. *Newsweek,* June 6, 1994.
8. Brandeis University Policy Center on Aging.
9. *Fortune,* May 17, 1993.
10. Betty Weiss story taken from *The Wall Street Journal,* April 10, 1995.
11. Bureau of Labor Statistics, 1993.
12. *Newsweek,* March 13, 1995.
13. Ibbotson Associates, 1993.
14. Ann Richards quote taken from *Women in Power: The Secrets of Leadership.* Dorothy W. Cantor and Toni Bernay with Jean Stoess, 1992.

About the Author

ESTHER M. BERGER is the author of *Money Smart: Secrets Women Need to Know About Money.* She is a certified financial planner, first vice president of PaineWebber Incorporated, Beverly Hills, and an internationally recognized expert on the subject of women and money. Her interest in women's issues has made her especially sensitive to the needs of her female clients, including single and married women, divorcees, and widows. She uses her professional expertise to help women overcome their fears about money and determine their own financial futures.

Ms. Berger is host of the PBS special *Women: The Financial Paradox* and a columnist for *Experience,* the magazine of the senior lawyers division of the American Bar Association. She is a frequent speaker to business and professional groups as well as to philanthropic organizations. At the invitation of the Pentagon, she addressed its Senior Professional Women's Association, which meets under the auspices of the secretary of defense, and was a featured speaker at the Smithsonian Institution lecture series.

Ms. Berger has been published in *Newsweek*'s "My Turn" and has been interviewed by CNN, *The New York Times*, *Los Angeles Times*, *USA Today*, *Forbes*, *Business Week*, *Money*, *Worth*, *Working Woman*, *Town & Country*, *Reader's Digest*, *Good Housekeeping*, *Ladies' Home Journal*, *New Woman*, *Marie Claire*, *Savvy*, *Success*, *Self*, *Cosmopolitan*, and News Limited Australia.

She lives in Beverly Hills with her husband, Leo, a certified public accountant, and their three sons.